Stop Landscaping, Start Life-Scaping

STOP
LANDSCAPING
START
LIFE-SCAPING

Hey CAROL Thanks for buying my book. I hope you enjoy the LiFE-SCAPING METHOD. MAY 2021 be a great year. Hope to see you. GARDEN ON! Monique

A Guide to Ending the Rush-rush, Humdrum Approach to Landscape Development & Care

MONIQUE ALLEN

Printed in the United States
First Printing, 2020

ISBN 978-0-578-61941-5

Developmental Editors: Kelly Malone & Susan Baracco
Managing Editor: Katie Elzer-Peters
Designer: Nathan Bauer
Copyeditor: Billie Brownell
Proofreader: Stephen Wilson
Cover Image: The Garden Continuum, Inc.

Dedication

This book is dedicated to two boundless forces in my life:

Mother Nature and her resounding abundance and resilience. She is by far the most amazing teacher by example. There is no arguing with her, there is only observing, responding, and making peace with what unfolds.

To my husband, Chris Allen, who introduced me to the resources of patience and stillness. Before he came into my life, I was anything but stationary. While to this day I have boundless energy to take on new ideas and adventures, it is Chris who continues to teach me by his example that settling in, staying for the long haul, and patiently loving and caring bring about the most amazing experiences.

CONTENTS

Introduction 1

   A Job, Turned into a Career, Turned into a Way of Life 1

Part I: Before You Dig In 19

   Chapter 1: The Landscape Connection 21

   Chapter 2: Why Systems Thinking Is So Important 45

   Chapter 3: The First Three Steps to Achieving Success in Your

   Life-Scape 73

Part II: Getting Started 91

   Chapter 4: Dare to Dream 93

   Chapter 5: See Your Setting 111

Part III: Digging In 127

   Chapter 6: Picture Your Plan 129

   Chapter 7: Build It 155

Part IV: Stewardship 181

   Chapter 8: Initial Survival 183

   Chapter 9: Forever Tweaking 203

The Garden Is Awakening 227

Appendix 231

Acknowledgments 235

About the Author 239

INTRODUCTION

A Job, Turned into a Career, Turned into a Way of Life

My introduction to gardening came at the age of 18. I was working at the local mall making minimum wage at T. Edwards, a now-defunct women's clothing store. I needed to work but as much as I loved clothes and fashion (and the discounts!), I didn't love my job. I craved the sun and real air, my feet were killing me by the end of the day, and I was so bored by the tedium of neatening up the displays that I could barely stay awake.

Plus, I couldn't bear standing around. I needed to move. Movement was important to my sense of well-being. I was a dancer, lifted free weights, and worked the Cybex circuit at the gym. I even taught aerobics classes for a short time; it turns out that was not my thing. Being used to moving, standing in a clothing store was not in alignment with my sense of self. I complained constantly to my girlfriends. I felt totally lost about what to do with my life. I didn't even have an educational aspiration yet!

One gorgeous spring day on my break I stood outside the store in the brightly lit walkway. I was trying to shut out the canned music, the constant stream of shoppers, and the aches in my feet that had migrated to my calf muscles. A new friend of mine whom I'd met in one of my college classes came up to me. "Hey Monique," he said. "What's up? Who died?" Yup, I had that look on my face. Being invited by his question, I proceeded to complain about my terrible job and how much I hated standing still and being indoors on such a gorgeous day.

"Why don't you come work with me this Saturday?" he asked. "We're doing a spring clean-up and mulching a property. I know my boss needs more hands."

I peeled myself off the wall I was leaning on and just looked at him. "Spring clean-up?" I really didn't know what he was saying to me, but it had something to do with another job and it sounded as though it would be outside!

He gave me a nudge with his elbow and said, "Come on, you'll like it."

Mulching? I had no idea what he was talking about. Landscape work and the language that went with it were totally foreign to me. I knew I loved being outside for sunbathing or swimming, but the closest I'd come to working the land was riding on my grandfather's tractor to haul water from the cistern. It was one of the most fun things about summer vacations at my grandparents' mountain vacation home. Still, I sure loved the expanses of land. So without really understanding what I was saying yes to, I shrugged and said to my friend, "Okay, why not?"

That Saturday morning was perfect for gardening. At 7:30 a.m., it was cool, still sweatshirt weather, with a clear blue sky. At the job site I felt the hint of warmth from the sun, a promise that my sweatshirt would be history in a few hours. The minute I got there I received a 15-minute crash course in weeding, edging, and picking leftover fall leaves out of shrubs. Later that morning, two big dump trucks backed into the driveway one at a time, and each dumped a load of mulch. I had never been close to mulch. I'd never even *thought* about mulch, let alone the task of mulching. The huge pile smelled like wood and earth, reminding me of being on the mountain with my grandparents. My job was to fill the wheelbarrows with mulch for the runners. What surprised me most was that the mulch was warm, even hot. A wave of heat poured from the pile as I loaded the first forkful into the wheelbarrow, which someone wheeled way. Almost instantly a new wheelbarrow appeared at my side ... the same side.

After I filled about four wheelbarrows, I realized I had to keep switching sides because I was "overtraining" my right side. I also needed to work my left side to stay even and not hurt myself. Lopsided isn't good for a bodybuilder or a dancer! I asked the guys to alternate parking the empty wheelbarrow on each side so I could load from the left, then from the right. I got some funny looks, but they humored me. As I worked on the pile that never seemed to grow smaller, I focused on engaging my lats, my shoulders, my traps, and my quads so that I was balancing my physical exertion with each movement. All the while I focused on keeping my belly engaged to protect my back, something I'd learned from doing squats. It was actually hard.

When you train in a gym, everything is set up to help you work muscles evenly because people tend to have a dominant side. Your goal is to balance the two sides of your body. In dancing, it is all about your center line and balance. In both, there is emphasis on form and stance as well as repetition. That wasn't the case with filling a wheelbarrow. It was repetitive all right, but not at all controlled. The angles were awkward, and I had to reach and stretch in a way you don't have to with a weightlifting machine or free weights. For the next two hours, I just focused on how to make the work useful to my body, not harmful. *Okay, how cool is this?* I thought. I was basically getting paid to train!! Plus, the sun warmed my back as I worked, filling me with a sense of joy that I'd never felt before.

Certainly not while working.

As the day wore on and the pile grew smaller, my new boss came over and asked if I would take on a new task. I felt fine with the change. I was feeling pretty hot and sweaty by that point, and I was tired, but I didn't let on. Seeing that I was the smallest person on the crew, he asked me to crawl under the larger shrub masses to spread mulch in places that a garden fork or hand couldn't reach. So on my belly I went and spent about half an hour spreading mulch in the shade, where I felt cool and protected from the heat of the afternoon.

At the end of the day, I was dirtier than I'd ever been in my life. I was tired and hungrier than the simple peanut butter and jelly sandwich I'd packed could satisfy. I felt giddy, happy, and even fulfilled despite my growling stomach. The boss counted my hours and paid me what turned out to be double what I made working at my "real job" at the clothing store. He said I'd done a great job for "such a little thing." This was the '80s and I was a teenager so he got away with that comment. Then he asked if I wanted to come back and work for them again the next weekend. "Hell, yes!" was basically my answer.

That gig was just a summer adventure with little potential for growth and after the first few weekends the learning curve leveled off. Even so, that job ended up being a great introduction to a career path I hadn't known existed. I wanted more!

My next gig was a step up the landscape ladder. I got a job working for a landscape architect who had designed and was now implementing a landscape for a residential compound consisting of a gated road with one main parent house and three family houses for the "kids." I worked on a planting crew. For a solid week we planted groundcovers, perennials, annuals, and dozens of planters of all shapes and sizes. It was on this crew that I met the woman who would become my gardening mentor for the next two years. She was well versed in perennials, garden design, and planting. In short, she understood how to bring beauty and vibrancy to a garden setting. She taught me a new way to think about nature and the outdoor spaces we call the "landscape." She introduced me to plants and their unique personalities, taught me about how colors work together, and how textures and forms can create beauty without a single flower. It was as though I was learning how to see the world all over again, looking at and interacting with the outside in a completely new way.

My life was rapidly changing. One hot summer day, I passed a tree on the bottom corner of my road, a Catalpa, although I didn't know that then. I looked up and saw these long, string beanlike pods hanging down from it. In a flash I realized they were seeds. Earlier that spring I had learned about the flower-to-seed cycle. I had never thought about trees having flowers, or seeds for that matter. These crazy 15-inch-long pods were almost shocking in their oddity. I jumped up to pick one off to see if I could learn what it was. And so began a lifetime of inquiring, "What is that?"

My feeling toward work was also changing. It was infused with energy, dialogue, excitement, and sometimes grueling labor. Since I was looking at the work through the lens of physical training, I was able to reframe what was hard into what could be seen as a tool to building my body, my muscles, and my overall physical capacity. This mindset was critical to my success because I ended up diving into this career choice with both feet, both arms, both legs, my shoulders, and my back. For the next five years, I balanced a full college workload with as much gardening as I could fit in. I even chose to garden for my spring and fall co-op requirements. I worked eight to ten hours a day, five days a week doing physical labor.

A couple of years later, after I graduated from Northeastern University with my BS in entrepreneurship, I was working on my own and continued to engage in physical labor for nine months out of the year. I kept that up for another ten years. Don't get me wrong; some days were seriously uncomfortable, like the day a bee stung me and my arm swelled up to my elbow. Or the time I got such a bad case of poison ivy my doctor ordered me to take a steroid to keep it out of my eyes. Or just the heat, humidity, cold, or rain, which made work harder than it needed to be. Even with all that, the beauty I encountered and the transformations I helped create made all that hardship fade away. There's an energy about cleaning and tending and planting in a landscape that feeds the soul as nothing else can. I also know the physical health I enjoy today, over three decades later, is in part due to my mindset of embracing gardening as physical training for all those years.

There were negatives in my new career choice, too, of which the biggest was the inconsistency in pay. No pay for rain days, no pay for travel time, reduced pay when the days got cut short. And back then, there were few landscape companies that offered any benefits. However, in those early years of internship when I was working toward my BS and training, I earned a good hourly rate for the time I was working. I loved the work, I was learning, and to be honest, I was having a blast, so I looked past the things about the job that weren't perfect.

As I became savvier in the garden, I came up with ideas about how to improve my employment experience, implement production efficiencies, and increase profits. I was embroiled in small business discussions on a daily basis at Northeastern, so I started pushing my mentor to make changes. I wanted to see her business amp up and evolve, and some of those changes happened. However, she was content to continue on her current path, so I knew it was time to strike out on my own. I was ready to develop a new business using the tools I was learning from studying entrepreneurship.

When I was 21 years old, in my third year of working as a gardener, I launched my freelance career. I continued to work for my mentor on several jobs, but I started taking jobs on my own as well. Even though my boss didn't want to pursue a partnership, we were still close, and she always encouraged me. At 22 I graduated from Northeastern and a few months later moved out of my mom's apartment into an apartment with two girlfriends. I was ready to make this career choice work. I felt as though I'd jumped off a cliff into the unknown, but that unknown felt so right that I never looked back for a second.

My gardening income wasn't enough to live on yet, so I was tending bar and waitressing to augment my income. One invaluable lesson my mentor taught me was that I needed to develop another skill, something that could be a stopgap to fill in the seasonal ebbs. With the help of my mother's contacts, I landed a great winter job at an accounting firm in Boston. Over the course of ten consecutive winters, I learned the basics of preparing taxes. I learned bookkeeping, data entry, and how to use an adding machine. I also transitioned that company from "pencil pushing" to a fully computerized tax prep system. For those ten years, I maintained my cash flow during the winter months when it was impossible to garden in New England. The skills I learned at the accounting firm became incredibly important tools to help grow my business.

As my business grew, I actively studied horticulture and

botany while working toward my graduate certificate in landscape design. I bought and read gardening books, in addition to my textbooks, to boost my knowledge of the industry. With every class I enrolled in and every book I read, I felt the weight of how much knowledge I needed to become accomplished in my profession. The good news was that while I was studying, I was also working with my own clients, providing the opportunity to test my new knowledge in real time rather than just absorbing the information theoretically. I learned about different plants and had several opportunities to engage with each one of those plants—to plant it, prune it, and even kill it. Trust me, the road to mastery in this profession is riddled with failures! Gardening isn't for the faint of heart.

When I learned a new design technique in class, I usually had a location to test it. It was a great way to learn because hands-on learning has always been my strongest learning style. Looking back, I now understand that hands-on learning is critical to skill building for everyone in this industry. You simply cannot gain the practical knowledge necessary from a book or a college curriculum alone. Intuition becomes important to the process and that comes from being connected to a practice for a long time. Get ready to get dirty in order to build the muscles in your brain and body that will guide you through the garden.

In my travels, studies, and my business, I seized every opportunity to learn and grow. I felt compelled to partner with local landscape contractors to get more work and generate better opportunities for myself. This was at a time when landscaping really meant mowing lawns, mulching, and maybe planting some shrubs and trees. Perennials were not as common in the trade as they are today, so I was offering something to these contractors that they didn't know how to do. I was dubbed the flower girl. Literally!

After one spring season, I became so busy that I hired other freelance gardeners to help me complete jobs. I hired my brother, his friends, my friends, friends of friends ... anyone who wanted to earn some money and wasn't afraid of hard work and getting dirty. I was driven and interested in seeing how far I could take this endeavor. I couldn't say no to a job. And let me tell you, that was both great and horrible! I wanted to take it all on and prove that I could make my business work. I am not sure whom I was proving it to, though; maybe it was to me. But it was important that this work meant something and that it could support me.

As a twenty-something I tended to move around a lot, switching apartments about every two years. From my perspective, every single apartment I lived in could benefit from some professional landscape upgrades. I would barter with my landlords to improve their landscapes with changes that would benefit them long after I moved out. Again, I couldn't help myself. I just always saw ways to improve my surroundings. Changing the landscape wherever I landed became as much a part of my apartment choices as it was a part of my daily living experiences. It was a long time before I realized that the changes I wanted to make weren't just for the sake of change; I needed to make these apartments feel like home. I was making them beautiful and comfortable, and that made me happy. Looking back, I see that I was sowing the seeds of Life-Scaping.

It may seem odd that during those ten years I spent so much of my spare time developing land that wasn't mine. But my apartment gardening also helped me get to know my neighbors, and I could see they were happy with the changes to the landscape. Everyone smiled when they saw me in the garden, and some neighbors even asked to help. It was the sweetest thing to come home and see a plant on my doorstep from a neighbor with a note reading, "I thought this would look pretty in your garden." I was living in the moment, improving those moments so that my living experience was more satisfying.

The first home I bought was a ranch-style house with an old, tired landscape. I went crazy ripping out ancient yews that had been sheared into boxes, overgrown rhododendrons that hid three windows and blocked all the light, and broken-down azaleas with barely a live branch left from having been totally squashed by the crazy rhodies and yews. I spent hours improving upon views by freeing up windows, screening out bad views by planting up the street edge, and adding fun plants like there was no tomorrow. I planted my very first Japanese threadleaf maple, a sweet-smelling 'Carol Mackie' daphne, and my very own Hinoki cypress. I felt as though I'd died and gone to heaven. I had planted all these plants before but never in my very own home.

That was just the start. In less than a year, I transformed that overgrown mess into a saleable home with a simple, yet beautiful, landscape that offered some privacy and beauty, where before it had been in total decline. I didn't invest a lot of time and money into the house itself, but I made some important changes. I ripped out all the old carpet and shined the floors, gutted and renovated a bathroom (vowing never to take on that type of project again), and painted every wall and every single piece of trim to make my drab house feel welcoming and bright. I soon sold this home in search of more land and a new adventure on my landscape journey.

And then I met Chris, my husband. When we became

engaged and decided to start looking for a house together, we drafted a list of the features we wanted for the house and the land. We ranked each item as a deal-breaker (gotta have that feature or no deal), negotiable (features that had some swing), and icing (if we could get it—sweet!).

On day one of house hunting, we found it! While the home inspector surveyed the house, Chris and I walked the entire 2.5 acres of land. Chris also happened to be a landscape professional and manager of a wholesale division of a nursery at the time. The poor realtor was so confused. Weren't we looking to buy a *house?* Why were we tromping all over the 2.5 acres of land? In our view, we were purchasing a homestead and if the land wasn't right then the house wouldn't work. Simple. Houses are either fixable or not, and I knew the inspector and felt he would give us the lowdown on the house's condition. But the land, that is another story. You aren't going to change the basic character and topography of the land. Oh, sure, it is possible, but enormously expensive. You are far better off starting with a piece of land that meets your long-term vision. So it stands to reason that you need a vision when you are shopping. And I wasn't short on vision.

We found a house that had all of our deal-breaker items, which was a details list. We made compromises in a few areas. As for icing, the house and land were basic without whistles or bells. But to us, both the house and the land were diamonds in the rough. We were purchasing pure potential, and we knew it.

The transformation began almost immediately in the form of gardening. It was years before we did much to the house. But the landscape—oh! We were all over that before the boxes were unpacked. It has been a work in progress ever since.

On the day we signed the papers, I started sketching and

journaling ideas about how we would renovate the house and the land. Chris and I talked about our house and the land all of the time. We loved to dream and plan our next moves. Sometimes we could plan for the short term. Other times it was years before we could bring a plan to life. Over time, we accomplished several project improvements on our land and made some big changes to our house. We moved the driveway to the west side of our land and tweaked the topography by adding two very large raised berms along the side of this new approach to screen it from the house. We raised the grade at the front of the house to create a terrace level above the main yard. We built a fabulous stone wall, added two granite steps through it, and fenced it in to make a wonderful courtyard garden. We built a patio, added dozens of garden areas, put in a pond, installed a well and irrigation system, and planted dozens of trees, hundreds of shrubs, and thousands of perennials.

Over a fifteen-year period, we also worked on the house. We built dormers, added two sheds and a garage with a loft, and then added a sitting room that included a full kitchen plus a bathroom renovation. We changed out every window in the house and installed a new heating and cooling system. With the exception of a few focal-point trees that existed when we bought the land and the woodland spaces surrounding the house, everything else on the property was moved from where we found it, redesigned, and installed new.

The point I want to make is that we had a vision and we worked that vision over time. We waited until we had saved the money or built equity in the house before beginning each project. The patio alone took three years. It has been an organic unfolding of ideas with each idea building upon the one before it. This vision could only come to be with planning, so we had to plan ahead. Sometimes it was the need for money that slowed down a project; at other times, we just needed help from professionals with the right equipment or skill set. We collaborated with one another and with other tradespeople as much as we collaborated with the land and the house. After we completed each project, we'd stand back and reassess the vision. We were "reading" the house and the landscape to see what was revealing itself as the next element we needed. We would have to balance the timing of the next project with our careers and with the demands of family.

As our professional lives and our family lives changed, so did our needs inside and outside the house. I wanted a playset for the kids that had never been in the vision. Now that it was, I had to convince Chris it was a good idea. Then we had to figure out where it would go. Of course, I had to find a particular set that fit with the look and feel of the house. Each phase of our landscape's development was tethered to where we were in our lives at that moment or in the moments that we could see unfolding. I feel blessed to have a partner in life who feels the same way that I do about how and why we make changes at home. We are responding to the dynamic changes in our lives so that we can continue to have an optimal experience of life.

Today our landscape and our home are truly Life-Scaped; they resonate with who we are and enhance our lives immeasurably. One way that I know they resonate is when I see my younger daughter lounging on our patio furniture reading a book or when she comes in with 100 pictures of flowers. I know it when my son comes speeding down the driveway on his bike and tells me I have to go look at the azaleas blooming because "They are so pretty." I know it when our oldest daughter decides to use our landscape as the backdrop to her high school senior picture!

All this comes with work. We have to manage it by taking time to maintain and tend many of the plants, but it is so beautifully aligned with our lifestyle that taking care of it is just part of the story. I would be lying if I said vacuuming my house was my favorite task but, boy, do I like my sitting room with my woodstove roaring hot after a good sweep and vacuum. It is so cozy and relaxing.

Gardens in a landscape are like rooms in your house; it's very much the same relationship. They take work and need tending to stay enjoyable to you. When gardens are well-planned, installed, and cared for, they become ecologically balanced. In time, most of our work is to keep Mother Nature from sneaking in too forcefully and tipping the balance in a direction that doesn't please you. I feel confident that, for the most part, the environment likes what we've done in our landscape because so many areas are thriving and require pretty simple upkeep. The design strategy was to ensure that many areas would become lower maintenance over time. For example, we have strong plant coverage that squeezes out weeds and keeps the mulching needs down. Other areas continue to be a work in progress because they haven't really settled yet or we just haven't given the focus and time to these areas. And we've had to renovate some of the earliest gardens because as the woods grow, so does the shade. We either have to cut down trees or we have to decide when a sun garden needs to become a shade garden. It is never boring, that is for sure. I can say that every person who's come to visit has felt the sense of balance and serenity on our homestead. In an aerial photo of our home, you can see how green and lush our land is compared to the neighbors on either side. No wonder the birds hang out here.

I believe we will be actively gardening for as long as our bodies allow. The heaviest work is done but there are always the yearly tasks to keep things in check and there's always puttering for fun. And if you are a gardener, life is nothing without a little dirt under your nails, sunshine on your back, and a new perennial cultivar to test out in your garden!

I am sharing my story because my introduction to gardening and landscaping was absolutely, positively life defining for me. After more than 34 years in this industry, it still amazes me how our environment speaks to and supports humanity. For me, gardening and landscaping have been a lifetime of work and inspiration and frustration, all of which has elevated my existence on this planet and my ability as a human being to manifest peace and beauty.

Hopefully, this book will help you connect the dots between the desire to own a landscape and the reality of having one. May you discover a new way of looking at landscaping and gardening. I want to demystify the process, debunk the myth that creating and maintaining a landscape is fast or easy, and inspire you with how fulfilling, joyful, and simple it is to put it all together. I also want to help you succeed rather than experience the sense of failure I see, such as the anguish about the good money spent on bad projects and the discouragement with all things landscaping.

My goal is to increase awareness both of the practices of landscape development and care (public and private grounds) and of the people who create and maintain these landscapes. These professionals are super important. I want to stress the value both landscapes and landscape professionals bring to the homeowner, the community, society, and the environment. I want to honor the people who choose this profession and those who choose to invest in this kind of work personally at their homes or publicly in their community because they are doing something much larger than just building a landscape. They are building, supporting, and fostering vibrant ecosystems, which in turn support the community. I want to elevate landscape work out of the anybody-can-do-it quick fix mentality perpetuated by television shows and restore all things landscape to the elevated status it truly deserves. I would like to give landscape work the recognition I believe it has earned for the incredibly important contribution that it is to our planet.

This book is a study in *why* more than *how*, an exploration of the underlying question of "Why does it matter at all?" Once you embrace why landscapes are so important, then the next step is employing systems thinking, understanding the web of relationships between all parts within a whole including the human factor and the patterns that emerge. I suggest reading this book from front to back to help you embrace a new way of thinking. You can then revisit any chapter at any time. Once you understand the *why*, the broad stroke of *how* will come through. At that point, you can revisit sections of this book and consult other resources for more detailed step-by-step directions.

Keep a pad of sticky notes by your side as you read this book so you can flag areas that interest you. For example, you might write, "Patio bases—why foundations are so important," and stick your note on that page. When you are ready to install your patio, you can reread the section you've marked to remind yourself of key points. That way you can have an informed conversation with your contractor or, if you are a contractor, with your client. That is when the book becomes a tactile, instructional, and useful tool.

I wrote this book for those who love gardens and landscapes. Often these are homeowners inspired to create something beautiful and functional for their personal use. I urge everyone who loves the landscape to engage in dialogue with their professional teams about how to approach a project, no matter the size, with a heightened awareness of how nature works. All of the players—homeowners, business owners, and landscape professionals—can implement systems thinking to care for the soil layer, to understand why planting sun-loving plants in the shade will lead to failure, and to appreciate why you might avoid buying a wooded lot if what you really want is an open, sunny one. Systems thinking protects us from mindlessly clear-cutting the forest as a way to make room for what we think we want in the moment. It helps us all to develop more awareness and to look to our past for needed wisdom and to our future to avoid unwanted consequences. At the end of the day, this book is for anyone who just really loves and is inspired by garden making.

PART I

BEFORE YOU DIG IN

You are ready to landscape your yard. The impulse is to go buy a pretty plant, grab a shovel, and dig in. I get it. I totally get it. But that is not how you start a landscape project. The process is similar to cooking a delicious holiday meal with all the seasonal mouthwatering flavors. You have to plan what you are going to cook, make lists, and order the tasks all before you put a forkful of food into your mouth. The French have a beautiful approach to cooking prep called *mise en place*, which means *everything in its place*. You've seen it on cooking shows, where all of the ingredients are prepped in advance, so the order of things is clear and access is easy.

Let's take the time to talk about the preparation work for your landscape project, starting with the overall concepts. Here's a snapshot of what we will cover in Part I:

- Debunk the current product-driven mindset of the landscape industry.

- Explore how a human partnership with natural systems makes so much sense.

- Look at how honoring those systems that we're part of can help us create a Life-Scape.

- Help you define your reasons for embarking on a landscape project.

- Identify whom you will partner with to get the job done.

- Help you understand your current environment so you know what may be changed.

At the end of Part I, I hope you will feel a sense of wonder and experience an "aha" around the different ways of considering the landscape and working within nature. The goal is to help you to define your reasons for embarking on your landscape project in the first place.

THE LANDSCAPE CONNECTION

"When we try to pick out anything by itself, we find it hitched to everything else in the Universe."

—John Muir, *My First Summer in the Sierra*

You are living in your dream home. Maybe you've been in your house for months, maybe years. It doesn't matter. You love it. You love the space, the floor plan, the remodeled kitchen with the six-burner stove and convection oven and the deep red bar stools that go with your super cool granite countertop. It is the end of the day and you come home after eight-plus hours of work perhaps sandwiched by a grueling commute. Or you return after chauffeuring the kids from school to soccer to dance class and send them upstairs or wherever to put away their stuff just so it is somewhere else for five minutes. You close the door behind you and take in your surroundings: your pictures, the walls painted the shade you worked so hard to find, the comfy chairs nestled up to the wood stove that will sit dormant for the next nine months now that spring has finally arrived, and you think, *home.*

The outside doesn't really speak to you, though. All of your hardscape features are in place. These are the elements such as a deck, a patio, a front walk, a driveway—the landscape features that are built and don't grow. And there's plenty of vegetation that includes a lawn, shrubs, and few perennials here and there popping up a little more each day as the temperatures warm. You might look at your yard through your living room or kitchen window, but you don't *focus* on your yard. You don't actually go *out* there.

And when you do? When you go out on the deck to relax with a cold drink, the deck bothers you. *I hate that railing,* you might say to yourself, or, *there's not enough room on my deck for the size table I want, or this deck is so splintery.* Or when you are on your patio, *It's too small* or *I need an umbrella.* So, the general feeling? It's bothersome and buggy. It's hot and weedy. It's this. It's that. You look at your landscaped yard and you think, *This place is a mess. I am goin' back in.* You haven't connected with the environment in a positive way. And part of that disconnect has to do with the evolution of landscapes into the one-size-fits-all solution. Today the landscape industry is a highly commoditized product-driven one that sets you up for failure. This book is meant to help you partner with your land, not with the big-box stores. Let the information in these pages help you connect with the landscape you create.

The Evolution of the Landscape

Being in nature, surrounding ourselves with trees, the sounds of birds calling, and the smells of the outdoors, is in our DNA. You've probably heard about or read studies that found contact with nature—such as plants, pleasing landscapes, and wilderness—can provide numerous benefits, including lower blood pressure and cholesterol levels, rapid recovery from surgery, and enhanced well-being. Nature is even helpful to children with attention disorders and teens with behavior disorders.

How did we get to a place where the outside is something we glance at through our windows from inside spaces? How did we get so disconnected? We need to look at the history of landscapes to figure it out. I am not talking so much about the beautiful scenery we admire from afar such as the red/purple mesas of the high desert, a wooded ravine, or the ocean, although if we love the feeling we get when we look at those landscapes, we may want to incorporate some similar elements in our yard. I am referring to designed landscapes.

Historically, the development of designed landscapes was reserved for the elite and wealthy who owned estates with multiple outbuildings. They had access to expansive tracks of land to develop between these segments of their homesteads, employing the highly accessible and affordable labor sources of the time. Sometimes the core features of these landscapes were used to highlight functions and features of the architecture. For example, tall trees anchored corners of buildings or low hedges directed the flow of foot traffic. There were fences to keep views channeled in one direction or to screen the working parts of the estate from one's view.

Courtyards for guest parking were critical for providing an arrival experience that would set the mood and tone for a visit or an event. Large lawns and patios nestled close to the interior entertaining rooms beckoned people to be outside in nature to take in the views and the fresh air. Much of what made estates grand was the incorporation of sweeping views and beautiful displays of colors and textures only found in the dance of plants in gardens. The landscape wasn't just something to look at or own, it was a place to show off class and style, it was a place to display art and craftsmanship.

Then came the development boom from the mid-1940s to the mid-1950s, when veterans returning from World War II and the Korean War needed places to live and landscaping gained traction with the masses. Post-war houses had a list of prerequisite must-have-to-sell features. Landscapes included a driveway for off-street parking, a walk to the front door, and often a small patio in the back. The lots had a patch of grass in the back for play and a patch in the front to create a neighborhood look. Beds with shrubs lined the foundation. And four saplings were placed in the yard: one in the center of the backyard, one in the center of the front lawn, and two on the parking strip each tethered to a stake.

With these post-war houses, architecture became plainer and more featureless. Think of the ranch- or Cape Cod-style homes that were prevalent during that time and continued into the 1970s. They were simple and functional but did not have much style in the features or the amenities. To be clear—I am not bashing either type. Of the two homes I've owned in my life, the first was a ranch and the second is a Cape Cod-style. The advent of these simple and affordable styles made owning a house possible for me. Along with that simplicity came new landscapes, which became more of a palliative fix or cover-up for the plainness and downright ugliness of new construction. For example, foundation plantings of the ubiquitous yews, rhododendrons, and azaleas that you see sheared into boxes, balls, and cones came into vogue when concrete foundations replaced the more expensive granite and natural stone foundations.

Time has watered down the purpose of the managed landscape and the green spaces we create for our homes and buildings. The purpose has shifted from being an invitation to be connected to nature, to get some fresh air, sun, and take a moment to rest and recharge to being an obligation for every architectural structure to include some greenery so it will sell. Ever heard of curb appeal? Essentially, it is the same as a window dressing, only it is on the outside.

We inherently connect with our environment using our senses. The managed landscape partnered with good architecture and thoughtful flow of features has the power to draw us in. One example is the arrival experience. How do you feel when you pull up to your house, park, and walk to the front door? What are you looking at? Is the journey beautiful, comfortable, and easy to navigate? Drive around and you will notice that this consideration has been deleted from the planning specifications. Nearly all human activity has been moved inside, and through the garage, no less. And the outside? It is an afterthought or it has become a playground for the latest fad feature.

New construction has lost the intention of the well-functioning outside space that includes nature for the express purpose of improving our human experience. What's missing? An easy-to-navigate driveway leading to a comfortable walking experience to the front door, and an entry landing big enough for more than one person. On the back of the home, we're missing a deck or patio big enough to entertain that connects in a smart and functional way to the inside of the house. Or decks and patios don't take advantage of views that have been framed to look at or screened for comfort without creating feelings of being penned-in.

As human beings, we have a necessity for connection to the outdoors. I'm not saying it's the same for all of us, but I am saying that being cut off from nature has negative effects that are becoming more prevalent in our society. The term *nature-deficit disorder* was coined by Richard Louv to describe these effects in his book *Last Child in the Woods*. While not a medical term, he used it to describe a phenomenon showing up in children who spent very little time outside. He says, "The future will belong to the nature-smart—those individuals, families, businesses, and political leaders who develop a deeper understanding of the transformative power of the natural world and who balance the virtual with the real. The more high-tech we become, the more nature we need."

How do we get back to a time when landscapes meant something more? Let's go back to the yard with the splintery deck. Only this time, you love your yard and your deck space. It fits, it is comfortable, and there are no splinters. You go out on the deck, maybe for a minute, just to check on the kids on the swing. You sink into a deck chair because you can't help yourself and you sigh. *I love it out here. I am getting a cup of tea, and then I am staying here. I don't want to leave. Ever.* Your experience is totally different. Your yard may not be any bigger. It may not be any more expensive. It may not have any different elements than the other one, but it resonates. I call this a Life-Scape. What's the difference between a Life-Scape and a landscape? A landscape is what you look at. A Life-Scape is what you live in. A Life-Scape resonates.

The Life-Scape

Life-Scapes share three distinct elements in their presentation: they are organized, they are healthy, and they have a little *wow* factor incorporated. Organization makes places easy to navigate. They make sense so we can rest our tired minds. Health and vitality in nature resonate through our cell structure to help us feel comforted and welcomed. This simply comes from being a part of nature ourselves. The awe and appreciation we feel when we are presented with high art, color, fragrance, sound, and enticing visual stimulation that draw us in to engage is what defines *wow* factor. It's the secret sauce that can take your landscape up a notch and stimulate a sense of joy.

Life-Scapes are to be actively and regularly lived in and visually pleasing because beauty is part of the experience, as is planning. Whether you do it yourself or hire someone else to do it, planning will be involved. The goal is to express and live your life in the context of nature. Engage with the process or you just won't be connected to your Life-Scape as fully as you could be. If you are managing your project and not doing the work yourself, then plan to be on the inside of that process, not on the outside looking in. Allow the relationship to blossom between you and the professionals with whom you work so that this insider experience evolves. If you are a do-it-yourself-minded person and you hire a professional here and there to lend a hand, you can still feel the satisfaction of completing the job by developing a relationship with the people who help you flow forward and make progress.

So how do you create a Life-Scape of your own? The beginning of your project requires a three-part planning process that may happen quickly or over many years, depending on the grandeur of your vision. The three parts are purpose, vision, and experience.

- **Purpose.** Define the functional uses that can be added to the outside spaces around your home as a way to improve how you live. Think about access from the inside to the outside, and outside to inside, think about playing and entertaining, enjoying solitude, and growing plants for joy or for food. Think of practical goals and consider parking, storage, privacy, and safety.

- **Vision.** Dream what the outside of your home could look like—think color, texture, levels, and even how it feels with the sounds and smells.

- **Experience.** Name three to five desired activities, events, or pleasures that you would like to have in your landscape over the next one to three years. Think about birthdays, graduations, and holiday events.

Here's an example of how this process works. Let's say you have had a home for about three years. You have a modest front yard and a good-sized backyard. Your kitchen door goes out to a small deck and a sliding door in your family room takes you out to a concrete patio. These two spaces are connected from different rooms in the house, but they don't really connect outside. Additionally, both your deck and patio are small and unwelcoming. Around these features, you have a yard that is a simple space with a few shrubs, flowers, and a lawn. The sun beats on the concrete of the patio, and the deck is made of pressure-treated wood that is becoming splintery. While both have functions and you can use them, they don't draw you out there to hang out. In fact, they are a bit repelling. Why is that? What's missing for you? Have you ever gone out there to really consider what's going on? What's not quite right for you?

You need to do that. You need to go out there and be with the spaces for a spell. Hang out there and ask, *if I could make this work, what elements would go away and what elements would come in?* If you don't feel you can be that specific, just list what bugs you about the space and why. This is how you start to define the **Purpose** of any landscape feature. And be patient with yourself because imagination needs patience to bubble up. Chances are you won't do this in one sitting. Making that list of what you don't like is the best first step. Really tear into what's not working and write that down.

After you've had your fill of hating on the space, now you will begin to exercise what I call your "want button," the place within you that is full of desires. This will be the seed of your **Vision**. Society, including our parents, teachers, bosses, and even spouses, tends to suggest quite boldly that wanting is bad. I'd like to give you permission to want, want, want it up in this visioning exercise. Don't censor yourself! Just like you listed what you hated, now list what you want. Here's the crazy thing: as you work this process you will start hating less and wanting less. It is just how this goes, and it's called honing your vision.

Now, imagine what you are doing and how you are feeling in this space. This is imagining the **Experiences**. Are you relaxed, are you partying with friends, are you cooking, gardening, sunbathing, reading? This list is endless. Write out a new list of these ideas. To round out this three-part exercise you will start to look for images that represent your purpose, vision, and experiences in magazines, books, online, and in your neighborhood or travels. It's impossible to have too much inspiration in these early stages of imaging your personal Life-Scape.

The beauty of this process is that it doesn't matter how much land, time, or money you have at your disposal. The process always starts the same way *and* when you embrace this process, your projects become effortless and enjoyable.

Landscaping: It Is All about Process

Why am I emphasizing the process? Because we've come to think of home repairs and landscaping as a quick fix anyone can knock out in a few days. And that is just not so. Something fundamental has happened to the garden and landscape industry since the 1980s, or before the superstores drove many smaller stores out of business. When I started in the business, my mentor and I used to go to a little garden center called The Family Tree on the VFW Parkway in Roxbury, Massachusetts. It was a really sweet place run by a father and his son with plants in the front and a mulch pile in the back. The dad was a true craftsman, a real veteran of an old-fashioned and highly connected way of landscaping.

Then a big-box store was built right behind their garden center—literally right behind their lot! Pretty soon, we'd start off at The Family Tree to buy what we needed but if they didn't have something, we'd pop over to big box to get the rest. But we always checked The Family Tree first; we were incredibly loyal. We loved these guys and really looked forward to visiting with them, not just because they were nice and friendly, but also because they knew stuff and they cared about what we were up to in the trade. But without loyalty, why would anyone choose this tiny shack of a place over the big, shiny big-box store behind it? The Family Tree eventually had to close, which was a truly sad reality.

Until big-box stores sprang up, access to the supplies you needed wasn't easy. Whether you were in the trade or doing a project on your own, you usually had to spend a lot of time finding what you needed. You went to one place and maybe they didn't have all the plants you wanted. If they *did* have the plants you wanted, they may not have the soil or fertilizer you needed. Or if they had the annuals and potting soil you were after, they didn't have the planters. You ended up going to six places just to get supplies for one day of work. But while you spent a lot of time, you also built relationships with vendors. They knew you. They remembered you, and often they'd even offer to carry a product line just for you. That connection is why it is so nice to go to small garden centers. Big-box stores have saved everyone a huge amount of time and made everything seem so easy to do. And quicker. And cheaper. Several sources, including *Inc.* magazine, *Statista*, and *BusinessWire*, report that the DIY market is exploding. It doubled between 2012 and 2018 and is on course to continue growing into the 2020s. Access to the tools and materials for DIY projects is unparalleled.

And if a DIY project isn't easy to do, the home improvement and garden television shows sure make it look that way. You can watch a quickie makeover that is done in an afternoon. This is unlike *This Old House,* which sprang to life well before the DIY boom and is still going strong 40 years later, where they devote a whole season to tracking the renovation of a home. They share all the ups and downs and complexities that truly occur during most projects. Now we can watch shows where a crew will come in and literally renovate a whole yard in a flash. It's a tiny yard, maybe 10 x 30, but viewers aren't thinking about that; they are thinking, *a new yard in five hours.* Anyone who's ever created a garden knows if you are landscaping a yard in five hours, even 300 square feet, you can only change the surface. But you've got millions of viewers fixating on a mantra of *five hours.* And that palliative fix goes viral.

The thing is, landscape development and care is not a project; it is a process from the initial vision to planning to implementing to stewardship, all of which I'll walk you through in this book.

The Landscape Demystified: Five Key Elements

For anyone who's ever attempted to garden and stuck with it for any appreciable duration of time, it is clear that it isn't so intuitive; you definitely need to do some research. For example, that research might include pinpointing what plants need in order to thrive or identifying some useful design elements to weave into a good plan. And it is never as easy or as simple as originally expected. You need to put your back into it. For example, there's heavy lifting and running around to get all the plants and materials you need. Before I scare you off with these bold statements, let's take a look at the disciplines that filter into and inform the landscape development process—art, science, organization, money, and labor.

ART

Gardening is an art. Designing is an artistic expression. As human beings, we need that expression. As Daniel Pink says in *A Whole New Mind,* "Design—that is, utility enhanced by design—has become an essential aptitude for personal fulfillment and professional success." Think about it. Even farms are laid out artfully. As you drive through farmlands, you may not see them as art, but when seen from a plane they are amazing stretches of fields networked with roads and irrigation. While we can look at art as freedom of expression and without boundaries or limitations, good art still has some rules. Granted, rules in art can be bent, pushed, stretched, and challenged, but the process—and result—is far more compelling when you know the rules first so that you truly understand what you are following or disregarding. On some level, this discipline is the easiest to play with, but it is still extremely important. And by learning a few concepts you can end up with a yard you absolutely love to be in. I hope that you will embrace the art of garden-making joyfully and even playfully. This is what makes landscape projects so much fun!

SCIENCE

Gardening is a science. Growing plants is an expression of life and all of the scientific processes that support life. I don't share this information to scare you, but rather to help you take a step back so that you can respect all that's going on in your plot of land. Knowing some of the science-stuff will help you to take a breath and slow down your project so that you get it right.

Broken into big chunks, these sciences are:

- Chemistry: science of matter

- Biology: science of living organisms

- Physics: science of matter and energy

Broken down further, we have these sciences:

- Soil Sciences – Pedology and Edaphology

- Plant Sciences – Botany (Agronomy, Forestry, and Horticulture)

- Entomology: insects

- Pathology: diseases

- Hydrology: water

- Climatology: weather

Every single garden on the planet is fully engaged in every single one of these scientific bodies of knowledge. If we were to look deeper into each area, we'd find that it would take several lifetimes to truly understand the full expression of ecology (relationships) in the garden. You should take comfort in knowing that there isn't a single landscape professional out there—designer, contractor, or scientist—who has a grasp on *all* these disciplines. That is simply not possible. In the landscape industry, professionals have a network of support from our partners, who can be vendors, fellow professionals, subcontractors, professional associations, and land grant universities. We have to be masters at reaching out for help, and you can do that too! There are wonderful websites available to supply you with information. In my company, we often use the UMass Extension website, to help steer our clients toward great tips. Some other favorites of mine are the Native Plant Trust's website and the Missouri Botanical Garden's Plant Finder website.

ORGANIZATION

Gardening takes planning. The most successful gardens are organized on a continuum between formal order and wild order. When you envision formal order, think of gardens that have lots of patterns and repetition, symmetry, lines, and geometric shapes that are easy to understand. When you think of wild order, think of gardens that flow and meander, asymmetry, fewer spaces between plants, and more organic shapes. There isn't a right or wrong to where your garden falls within this spectrum, but to be organized is to maximize value and reward.

From my years of experience in many facets of the landscape profession and personal gardening endeavors, I know that to ease frustration and increase your chances of success, you need to approach the land with a plan that has a beginning, middle, and end. Haphazard doesn't pay out, and it usually costs you in the end! Why do we think organization comes naturally, simply, or easily within the practice of gardening?

The do-it-yourself (DIY) movement has been a blessing and a curse to our understanding of the importance of organization in landscape project planning, development, and care. The curse comes from the idea that anyone can do just about anything in the landscape at any time. I think that for any endeavor, certainly not just landscape projects, that simply isn't a truth that I can wrap my head around. When you take an art form, especially one with so many ties to science and the environment, and you try to distill it to make it accessible to the masses, you lose something in that process. What I, as an academically trained and field-seasoned professional, see is that many people struggle with how landscape development works and then find themselves frustrated, or worse, they make costly mistakes. While most people can follow simplified steps, what gets lost is the underlying reasoning and structural functions behind those steps. My hope is this book will demystify some of those nuances that may make a project a little more complex, but which will also ensure more successes.

It must also be said that the DIY movement has been a blessing. I believe with every ounce of my being that the desire to work the land is innately and inextricably part of being human. While people feel this to varying degrees, it is clearly somehow interwoven in our DNA. When easy access is granted to the tools and supplies as well as to information, it liberates people from all walks of life to pay attention to these yearnings and then to, in fact, "do-it-yourself." That's super cool! That truth has elevated the industry into the common language of the building trade, the real estate market, and to homeowners of every socio-economic class.

Here's what's troubling to me: when something complex is stripped of those dynamic details and spread out over all economic and marketing channels, it can't help but become commoditized and then marginalized. What was once revered, becomes common. What was once a profession, becomes a pastime. Art and science get stripped down to basics and what we end up with is what feels to me like a cheap, throwaway, product-centered, quick-fix approach to something that deserves far more respect and appreciation.

My enduring question has become, how can we have both? How can we elevate this amazing work of landscape development and care as an important part of our human experience while also keeping it accessible to all who are eager and interested in doing work themselves? The answer I've landed on is awareness. If we *know* that organization is paramount to success, then we'll seek it out and learn it, or find someone to help who knows about it. When we land on the truth that landscape work—whether it's a small garden project or a major landscape development—is not a simply a project, but, more accurately, a process, we will invariably choose to plan ahead and thereby make better decisions.

MONEY

Gardening requires some financial commitment. It goes without saying that all landscape and garden endeavors take some level of investment. Just like there is a continuum of organization as described earlier, there is also a financial continuum that requires consideration. The key is to get clear on your starting point land conditions and then clarify where you are trying to end up. The work becomes trying to tease out what the monetary investment will be get from point A to point B. And, just as a caution, I'll state that landscape projects—especially renovations—tend, in my experience, to take more time and money than folks expect. With that in mind, I'll share some thoughts on how to think about the money component of landscape planning, development, and care.

Every element in your landscape from the built hardscape features (like a patio, or pool, or wall) to the plants you choose and the soil you prepare will need to be designed, constructed, and planted to last. This means that the process of planning a project, especially larger ones, can come with some associated costs. It could be as simple as buying this book, or more involved like taking a class, or you may find that hiring a consultant or a designer is the way to go. This is because things like solid foundations, especially in the colder climates, are important design considerations for the constructed elements of your projects (the hardscape). It means plants need to be selected with your specific site and geographical location in mind. And, understanding your soil structure before the planting design starts will help you understand what you're working with so that you are able to make modifications that make sense (the greenscape).

Maintenance is no less of a financial consideration. I've seen beautiful landscapes that get installed only to unravel over the years because of poor follow-up care. If maintenance is not considered in the initial capital investment or the ongoing operating costs of your landscape, it can lead to failures and future expenses that could be avoided. My company was invited to design and lead the landscape installation portion of an episode of *Extreme Makeover: Home Edition* held here in Medfield, Mass. It was both hell and the most fun ever. But that poor family! As soon as that show bus packed up and left them the real story started. We realized very quickly there was no way they could manage the landscape they received. They didn't have the time, expertise, or money. We worked to organize further donations of landscape products and services in that first year to help them out. We lined up snow plowing and mulching, and we gardened for them to keep things from becoming inundated with weeds. But even with that help, they couldn't manage. We continued to help for four more years until the landscape became more mature and easier and less expensive to maintain. At that point, they took on some care themselves and hired a local landscape firm to do the basics for them. TV doesn't tell that story!

The important lesson from this experience was to bring up the discussion about maintenance much earlier in the planning process. By doing this, I am able to engage my clients in a substantive exploration of what it means to have ten thousand square feet of lawn area. What will it need in terms of mowing, watering, fertilization, and pest and disease management? Lawns are not native here in Massachusetts, and they can be costly to maintain. Knowing that upfront can help drive design decisions. It makes no sense to build a landscape that will outstrip your resources now or later, so working from the finished product care elements backward is a great exercise to engage in with your landscape partners.

LABOR

Gardening takes effort. "Easy" is not a word I would use to describe landscape development or even gardening. I laugh as I write this because I've been doing this kind of work for so long, that I don't focus much on the fact that what I do is "hard, manual labor" anymore. It's just what I do! But, I can say that from being an employer as well as a service provider in this field of work, I've seen people entirely out matched by the physicality of the work of tending the land. It is something that can be surprising to those diving in for the first time. And, after all these years of work, I have my own personal set of aches and pains that I believe are a result learning to do this work before there was much talk about personal safety or ergonomics to prevent injury. The caution is simply this: take care of yourself because injuries are a drag, to state the obvious!

An important distinction about this work is that it occurs within a living system that includes plants and soil so it's best to approach both with the care you would offer a beloved pet. I am not saying that you will develop the same attachment and apply exactly the same level of care to your peonies as you would for your poodle, although some do. It's best to approach landscaping and gardening with the understanding that there is caring and work involved. Most people tackle their landscapes with more willpower than purpose or planning. Willpower is fine to a point, but it won't get you far for long. In fact, studies show that willpower is in short supply unless there exists a deep meaning and purpose behind whatever we are calling on willpower to get us through. Simply put, we only get a little bit of it every day, and it is not meant to get us through the long haul. It is there to get us started, push us over a hurdle, and help us create good habits. We can't build or manage a landscape on sheer willpower alone. We need to have more connection with the landscape and our investment in it.

After embracing the art and science embodied in landscape work, it's hope and faith that takes us the rest of the way with a bit of willpower to push us over the real hurdles. Here's an example. Let's say you've designed a meditation garden, and in it, you plan to have a flowing garden that will attract pollinators with a small water feature for the sounds of water, a tiny patio with a comfy bench to sit on, and a touch of lighting so you can use the space in the evenings if the spirit moves you. Just reading this sentence you can connect to the art, the science, and the organization of the space. Now you have to build it, piece by piece. When you start digging the water feature and hit a ton of rocks, you may feel defeated, so you call upon willpower to keep laboring through. What gets you back out there the next day to keep working that hard? You may say that is just more willpower, but, in truth, it is the hope you have that your meditation garden dream will come to be and the faith you have in your ability to build it.

WHAT CAN YOU RELY ON?

When you look at a garden as an art expression that is tethered to science you will begin to grasp the complexity of larger projects. My hope is you will believe that organizing your project in advance through the art and science lenses will help you to prepare for success. Then, when you add the resources of money and labor into the mix, you'll get even closer to outlining a project that you know you really can accomplish, either on your own or with a professional partnership.

That's when you will start seeing results. Don't lose your hope, faith, or your willpower; you are still going to need those important tools! When you conserve willpower to carry you through the hard times and use your brain, intellect, and good old ingenuity in the day-to-day, then you are flush when the locusts come. And oh, they will!

Understanding the landscape process is really recognizing all the disciplines and elements involved. I am not trying to scare you off or overwhelm you. You don't have to master each area to create a beautiful yard you love. You don't need to be a chemist or biologist, or hold a degree in horticulture or fine arts. You just need to have an awareness of what is involved. This awareness is the tool you need to drive you toward asking good questions. It is the questions you have that will point you in the direction of success *more* than the answers.

Just think about it this way: If you were taking medication and your doctor told you to take another medication in addition to the first, wouldn't you be curious about the interaction between the two? What if a third were piled on? Would you pop that pill without considering the side effects? When you treat your lawn, you need to ask questions about the effects any products have on the ecosystem because it isn't only the grass you are treating. First, *everything* you put on the lawn also goes into the soil. The microbes in that soil are being treated, for better or for worse. The product you put on your lawn also affects the water in that living system. That water is mobile, meaning that the product may be carried to the aquifer and waterways. If you are using a spray, those small particles you are spraying don't just land on your grass; they are carried on the air to other areas and possibly into your lungs. I am being very simplistic here, but hopefully, you are getting the message of relationships. Everything is connected to everything else.

***

In the next chapter, I will discuss another partnership—your partnership with the land and vegetation because you are dealing with living systems, not just products. Then we will look at how you engage in the process to help you determine what you *really* can or cannot do. Maybe you will like building patios, decks, fences, but will not like digging, weeding, pruning, or mowing your lawn. I'll help you determine when it is best for you to partner with experts, and how to choose and work with those experts.

TODAY'S TASKS

1. Identify your project area and make a list of all the things you want to accomplish starting with what you hate about the space, why you hate it, and why you want it to be different.

2. Make your first list of elements you would like, why you want them, how you will use them, and what is important about them to your home life. This will be the start of your research list.

3. Decide on how much you want to invest in your project. Your time, labor, and money. Remember, until you have a design, it's impossible to get a true price but at this moment, you probably have an idea of what you feel able to invest. Start there.

WHY SYSTEMS THINKING IS SO IMPORTANT

"We are told that the trouble with Modern Man is that he has been trying to detach himself from nature. ... Man is embedded in nature."

— Lewis Thomas, *The Lives of a Cell*

Landscape development, whether it is an intricate master plan or a simple garden space, requires that we apply the natural sciences to achieve success. We need to think about soil, plants, sun exposure, access to water and all the things that make a landscape grow and thrive. We need to think about all of the relationships including our role in the game. But even taking these elements into account, the landscapes we construct are not natural. What do I mean by that?

As soon as we start dreaming about landscape design, big or small, and start devising ways to lay out the beds, plants, stones, and mulch, we're toying with the natural ecosystem. Even when we create our landscape with species native to our region, we're bringing considerable human intervention into what would otherwise be a less organized, less managed, less diverse, and maybe even less appealing world. Human intervention isn't a bad thing. Mother Nature has her own agenda to cover the land and to allow natural ecological succession. Her goal counters our residential or even commercial agendas for an environment managed for human comfort and enjoyment. So when our plan is to emulate nature, we want the *look* of natural in its most organized and pleasing form. However, it is important to understand that as soon as we stick our hands in Mother Nature's business it is no longer natural, and it is very hard to walk away. And since Mother Nature never sleeps, we have to maintain the landscape we created or natural succession will alter our intended design. The point is to fully own our participation in this endeavor from start to finish.

The Greenwashing of an Industry

Our commercial landscape industry would like us to believe that we can go natural, that we can step in line with how the Big Green Mama creates something that is natural and native and that can ultimately be left to its own devices. That, in essence, once we've purchased all the right plants and products and installed them all, we can leave them alone, just like in nature. It appears, if you watch or read mainstream home-improvement media, that maintenance is a dirty word to be avoided like the plague. The easy, turnkey, set-it-and-forget-it dream is really just that—a dream. While we are misled about maintenance-free landscapes, we are also misled about the work needed to keep these planted environments vibrant and pleasing in the long term. We are being "greenwashed." Whether by accident or on purpose, our environment is being oversimplified and commoditized to ease our mental burden and concerns over how to deal with it. The truth is, every constructed landscape needs care in the beginning as well as some level of attention indefinitely whether it's a residential, commercial, or public-use space. There are few plants that simply fit where we plant them for all eternity, especially if there are structures in the mix. Plants grow, they fall over, they get sick, they reproduce. If we just leave our landscapes alone, we will have chaos.

At the same time, we are being coerced into believing that repeatedly mulching a landscape, shearing shrubs, and pruning trees to fit is somehow helping us create a representation of the natural environment. But that is not true either. It is a representation of the attempts of humans to subjugate nature. So why the greenwashing? On the one hand, I think it is because we freak out when plants get too big and feel the wild is taking over, so we need to tame them. On the other hand, we feel better if we think we are doing something natural, something that would happen in nature without us. Maybe we feel we are being kinder to the earth. The industry and the media are responding to this need to tame the wild while helping us to believe what we are doing is natural, and we are responding with our purchasing power.

Taking Cues from Nature

"Natural" implies existing in or *caused* by nature, not made or caused by humankind. On some level, we want to mimic the most successful and the prettiest constructs of nature. That means we are working within a proven system and duplicating the awe-inspiring effects of nature. We are taking cues from how nature is organized and how it functions and saying, "Ooh, if I do *that*, then I could have *this* outcome." A historical design goal was often to recreate the natural landscape exactly, but often those designs were for extremely large tracts of land.

Take someone like Frederick Law Olmsted and his work that's represented at the Arnold Arboretum of Harvard University in Jamaica Plain, Massachusetts. When you walk through that landscape, you feel as though you are in a totally natural topography. The roads suggest humans, but the hills and valleys, waterways, and majestic trees all drip with the essence of nature. In fact, they are not at all natural. Olmstead built every hill and valley. He mapped the roads and then planted all the trees. He even planned how to use the water found on this site; this was back in the day when you were not restricted in manipulating waterways. His landscapes are a work of pure visionary genius. It is said that Olmsted had a 40-year vision. He imagined how the plants would look in the future after they filled out and matured. He designed with those enormous tree trunks and canopies in mind. He even planned for the competition the roots would create. He was working on this sun-drenched site, but he was designing for spaces that would be in the shade in the future.

With that kind of vision, you are planting with the understanding that your future design goal may kill all the sun-loving plants that you used for filler while the trees grow to their mature size. It is so cool to think about how Olmstead's mind developed the layout of that beautiful arboretum. Few of us have that level of design sense when it comes to crafting space using living, breathing elements. Applying the principles of nature and natural succession to create an environment that so closely resembles a work of Mother Nature is a rare skill. And don't be fooled; Mother Nature does take over, eventually. On some level that is the goal: to jumpstart a natural system with your vision as the leaping-off point.

Aiming for a landscape inspired by nature is the right

approach, as with the Arnold Arboretum. But as a homeowner, you must keep in mind that when working in a residential space, you are limited. You have to take the cues from nature and then convert or adapt them to the confines of a small residential lot. Nature-inspired design may speak to plant communities and plants that are naturally found together that make good bedfellows in your landscape. Tree choices that mature to a size that will fit your landscape fifty years from now are a great choice, even if in fifty years the site is shady where it is now sunny. We need to think about using the genius of nature and overlaying that into our constructed landscapes.

In some places, nature-inspired design can be impractical. Take a home's foundation planting, for example. We may select plants that are well suited to the environment, but then we plant them in an ordered fashion alongside the house or in the yard. We are neat about it because we like things lined up, spaced out, and arranged in a certain way. But nature would not go to all that trouble. She would toss the plants in a haphazard or natural way and allow the plants to duke it out for survival. That result isn't generally what we would call curb appeal.

Landscape Versus the Wild

The average person is uncomfortable with the wild because it has bugs that bite us, prickers that snag our clothing, and wild creatures that give us nightmares. Then there are plants such as poison ivy, poison oak, and poison sumac that can make us itchy. On the other hand, people love areas that have been landscaped, whether it is a simple cleared trail or a fully manicured garden. Clearly, there's a continuum of how heavy the human hand can be on the land from the highly manicured to the loosely arranged and lightly managed. And there are some who can blaze their own trails and turn their front yard into a completely edible garden. For those of us interested in building an outside environment where we can hang out, a big part of the effort is how to keep the wild *out*, say on a lawn, or on a patio, or even snuggled up to a fire pit, in an effort to be comfortable.

In more than three decades practicing as a landscape professional, I have yet to meet a client interested in a completely wild landscape. I guess if they were, they wouldn't be calling me in the first place! But I have certainly encountered many who were interested in a native landscape. They are often inspired by the conservation movement that took hold after Rachel Carson's book *Silent Spring* was published in 1962 and the government bodies that protect water resources were formed.

Building a Native Landscape

Going back to the example of the Arnold Arboretum, those hills and valleys took tons of earth moving to create, not to mention some serious heavy lifting. Then to make the hills and valleys look as though nature had built them, they needed many plants, from seedlings to larger transplants. And then a concerted effort was needed to care for the new plantings. Later, care was needed to keep the native landscape from returning to the wild. I am not trying to steer you away from a natural-type landscape, but I am simply painting the scope of the effort required. Just because you choose to plant native species doesn't mean you are spared the upfront work of planning, designing, installing, and maintaining the landscape as it acclimates and establishes. Building a new ecosystem is upfront work no matter the style. It is on the back end or the maintenance side, as the landscape matures, where a native-style design can save you work.

When my husband, Chris, and I moved into our home the very first thing we wanted to do was to move the driveway. This was a 200-foot, stick-straight driveway from the street to the house. It was boring, uninviting, unimaginative, and it didn't look the least bit natural. It looked and felt like a runway!

To create a natural look we wanted, we followed these steps:

1. Laid out the template for the new driveway in its new location using four lengths of 100-foot hose.

2. Added two nice curves into the driveway to make it meander.

3. Drove the new layout of the driveway right over the lawn to see if it worked. Yes, we literally drove on the old lawn—which was all weeds anyway.

4. Dug the new driveway out with heavy earth-moving equipment in its new location on the west side of the property.

5. Built two large earthen berms using three hundred cubic yards of soil on the east side of the driveway to screen it from our front yard and the views from the windows in our house.

6. Bought hundreds of plants and planted them on the berms.

Phew! But, boy, is it a pleasure to drive into our property now. The berms are as beautiful from the driveway as they are from the yard. We even built a pond into one of them, though I'm still working on bringing out my inner Olmsted. Now we have a bendy, curvy drive that wends its way past hills and trees and a pond. The cool thing is while we work in these areas every year, they are still some of the lowest-care areas in our landscape. Honestly, the lawn is more work than these enormous berm plantings.

A newcomer to our home has no idea what it took to build that driveway, nor do they understand what it took to nurture it to maturity. What they see is an almost effortless landscape on which Chris and I do far less work now. It requires some seasonal weeding, some mulching from time to time, and some pruning. Since then, we have also had plants taken out by storms that had to be removed and replaced or "loved" back into shape.

Partnering with the Wild

My home sits on 2.5 acres. The entire back, which is just over an acre, is woods and the entire front acre is the house and landscape. But even our woods are not fully wild. We maintain them. We cut path we can drive on and installed a compacted stone base to keep it firm. We planted an entire set of understory plants beneath one area of huge pine and oak trees. Early on, we culled some trees and cut back the underbrush to make the woods feel more open and vibrant. As the older trees decline or die, we clean things up to encourage new young trees to mature and take over, always leaving some to decay to become food for insects and birds. And every four or five years, we brush-cut the undergrowth in the woods, knocking down the ferns and the blueberries so when they reemerge the following year, they remain as a low groundcover. This effort offers up a gorgeous space in nature allowing Lady's Slippers to proliferate in their preferred conditions.

We walk our dog there every day. The kids even used to sled back there in the winter when they were little. But it is not fully natural, trust me. Or ask Chris, who does all that work! As I walk out there now, I see poison ivy and bittersweet taking hold in pockets. Suddenly, I am seeing black swallow-wort and garlic mustard moving in, which are two emerging plant problems in our area. This may be my fault; some of the work we have done let these invaders in. I'm curious to better understand the exact causes for this shift in my landscape. What I do know is this woodland is a constantly evolving ecosystem that requires a vigilant partnership to manage well.

Wherever there is a trail system, there is usually some level of maintenance involved, especially on the trails themselves. Someone has to prune the tree branches off the trail. If the woods are inside the city limits, that area is usually managed by a city department such as Parks & Recreation or an Open Space Committee. The town of Franklin has a forest management plan, and our conservation commission hired a consultant to draft this plan, which is filed and valid for ten years. When I was a member of the conservation commission, we gave permission for the town to hire a logging firm to cull trees according to a detailed plan. This plan allowed us to properly manage the forest for the long-term health of the remaining trees and for the overall stability of the woodland. The logging company cut and cleared invasive species, tangled brush, and understory along with large pines, maples, and oaks that were labeled as weak or damaged. Trees that were crowding other trees were also removed to guard against larger losses.

While we don't have forest fires here in New England like other parts of the country do, this work is critical for being able to manage a forest fire should one occur. Because the town used a logging company to do the work, they harvested the wood and reaped the financial benefits. Still, a lot of people were really up in arms about the work because they didn't understand the idea behind managing the woods. They felt that the woods should be left natural. But what they didn't understand is that "natural" in the truest sense means humans are 100 percent hands-off. This approach would cause those woods they cherished and loved to walk in to become thick and impassable. Even my measly one acre of woods wants to go wild every time I turn my head. We won't let it because the majesty of those trees and that space is elevated through our care.

There is indeed a place for wild nature but most of the people who voiced concern said they liked the woods as a place to walk on trails and enjoy nature, which is a managed woodland. As stewards of this forested land, cleaning the woods used by so many townspeople was the right course of action for the conservation commission. A level of managed control is necessary, and this is how we manage woods so they are safe for people. This is how we partner with nature so everybody wins. In the case of the woods in my town, the lumber company got the wood, the town benefited financially, and the population has beautiful, safe woods to walk and enjoy.

Understanding Living Systems

To partner with nature, we need to understand how it works and the living systems involved. These are self-organizing living things that interact with their environment and are maintained by a flow of information, energy, and matter. And we need to understand our part in that entire system. We've raised our awareness in so many parts of our lives. We have developed skills and amassed tools such as incorporating healthy foods into our diets, fitting exercise into our weekly schedules, and visiting our doctor regularly. All of this is done in the name of living long, productive lives to leverage our work efforts and our earning power. We are interested in improving our life experience by being mindful in all that we do. If we approach our gardens in the same way so our experience in the garden and in nature informs and enriches all parts of our lives.

But first, we need to understand how gardens work, which is not all that different from how we work. Anybody can make over a yard by rolling out some sod, filling a bed with annuals, or planting a tree. But you are not working with the natural system of how plants and soil and the surrounding environments depend on one another to thrive. If you don't work within the system, then your new landscape is not sustainable. A quick makeover is an *applique*, something you just put on top of the land; it isn't really connected. Think of a landscape makeover in terms of your own body. We can easily do a makeover, right? A little makeup, a haircut, a change of clothes, and voilà—we look different. But are we different?

QUICK FIXES FOR OUR BODIES

Let's go deeper.

You take an aspirin when you have a headache but what you really need is to drink water because you are dehydrated. Maybe that is why you get the headache every day at the same time of day. Because after three cups of coffee, your body is yelling, *Cripes. Will you please hydrate my brain with some*

H2O! I speak from my own over-caffeinated experience here.

I am not suggesting we steer clear of quick fixes entirely (or coffee, for that matter). I am not telling you curb appeal is a bad idea; throwing in a couple of annuals without a lot of thought is okay. Trust me; I've done it and will likely do it again. Placing a couple of planters filled with tropical flowers and foliage that won't winter over on your front steps is fine. Planters are one of my favorite kinds of summer plantings. That's where I stop, though. Using synthetic fertilizers to feed your lawn to get it to green-up fast might be a way to make it look more vibrant in the moment. However, if your lawn has low organic matter, thin soil, or compaction, which happens when the delicate honeycomb of air and water pockets in the soil that support all the microbial life in that area is crushed, then applying a quick fix of nitrogen to your lawn is the same as eating a candy bar when you are hungry. It does the trick in the moment, but in an hour, you are either going to crash from the sugar or become ravenously hungry.

We all apply quick fixes. We all pop an aspirin when our head is killing us, slap on some concealer when we haven't slept, or smile when we are definitely not feeling happy. When we look at the bigger holistic picture, we must treat our bodies and the environment we live in as living systems, integrated parts that function in unison.

QUICK FIXES FOR THE SOIL

Let's talk soil. We are, mostly, building dead-scapes, not Life-Scapes, with the way we disregard soil. I don't think people are out to do any harm, but, rather, they don't know that harm can be done. Compaction is the first assault on the land, which is almost irreparable. If there is no life in the soil, that upper layer of earth where plants grow called the rhizosphere, there can be no life *anywhere*. In order to have the ecologically functioning landscapes we want, we must avoid thinking about the soil as inert or as lifeless dirt. While the words "soil" and "dirt" are often used interchangeably, they are actually polar opposites. Simply stated, "soil" is full of life. The book *Teaming with Microbes: A Gardener's Guide to the Soil Food Web* by Jeff Lowenfels and Wayne Lewis is a great resource if you want to dive more deeply into understanding soil.

Soil is filled with oxygen, water, and minerals, which are used by a diverse population of microbes. The interaction between these resources in the soil creates nourishment for the plants. "Dirt" is dead. There is no life in dirt. Dirt is what you find caked to the bottom of your boots and on the knees of your pants at the end of the day. Dirt is what you find on the floor of your car and in the corners of your mudroom. The life is gone because the water has dried up, the microbes have died, and there is no structure to hold oxygen. When we approach the soil as dirt, it is easy to tromp all over it without care or thought. But if we consider an entire microcosm of life beneath our feet, we'll tread lightly with both care and respect.

Another way that soil is damaged is through the repeated use of synthetic fertilizers, which feed only plants. Over time, the soil microbes will suffer from lack of nutrients, making it harder to maintain lush, green vegetation, even with those fertilizers. There's an old gardener's adage that goes, "Feed the soil, and the soil will feed the plant."

THE WHOLE VERSUS PARTS

One of the reasons it is such a hurdle to think of a landscape as a living system is because we don't think of *ourselves* as living systems. The modern medical profession has shifted our reality so that we think of ourselves as a collection of parts. We have a heart and it has a doctor. We have lungs and they have a doctor. We have reproductive parts and a doctor for those. We have a brain and about six different doctors for that crazy thing. Visualizing the landscape as a whole can be tricky when we see ourselves as a bunch of independent pieces. As a culture, we are geared to treat these independent parts of our bodies and our landscapes with products. We take aspirin for an aching head and apply fertilizer to a pale green lawn. The products aren't bad in and of themselves, but, rather, they are a quick fix more like a topical Band-Aid. They don't address the underlying cause of the issue.

And in a product-driven market where you apply a quick fix here and quicker fix there, you become beholden to the next product that will be used to treat your next problem. Take fungicides for lawns; each year *pounds* of fungicides are sold and applied to lawns. As soon as people see a fungus, usually after the humidity sets in, their knee-jerk reaction is, "What product can we use to fix this?" when the real question should be, "What underlying cause is making fungus grow in my lawn?" Fungus overgrowth has connections to a whole host of other things that are happening with your lawn such as watering practices, poor air circulation, and humidity. Just throwing fungicide on it is not going to change those underlying causes or fix anything permanently. Instead, you will find yourself in a predicament of always having to apply fungicide on your lawn because you are not solving its true problem. See how this is product-centered? Good for the market, bad for your lawn. Ultimately, you are medicating the lawn along with the soil and all the biology that lives there so this method isn't sustainable. It sets you up to spend more money over and over again.

The best correlation is the use of antibiotics. In the mid-twentieth century, we began using antibiotics for everything. By the time we entered the twenty-first century, we were beginning to understand the issues of antibiotic-resistant bacteria and realized that by overmedicating, we were creating new and stronger strains of bacteria. This is science in practice, meaning there is nothing *exact* about it. It mutates and evolves along with us. Our job is to be vigilant in our awareness and responses. Simply put, if we overmedicate the body or the environment, we end up in a lesser state of health than when we started. We have effectively weakened the terrain so the host can no longer fight the invader on its own.

If you apply a control chemical or even an organic chemical, you have to be clear about whether you are solving a problem for good or temporarily masking it. Both a temporary fix and a permanent fix have their place. Sometimes a permanent fix would be great, but it isn't possible; that's when a temporary fix is needed. Additionally, it is important to note that some fixes are for mistakes that we have made in our gardening, while others are somewhat out of our control.

For example, let's say you love the look of *Pieris japonica* and you plant three on either side of your front foundation of your home, which faces roughly east. The nice morning sun is perfect for these plants, which would prefer not to be in the hot sun. In a couple of years, you notice that the ones on the northeast side of your foundation are doing great, growing thick and lush, while the three on the southeast side of your foundation, especially the one on the very end, seem stunted, yellowed, and thin. What's up? A landscape company will tell you that the plants have a lace bug infestation and the fix is to apply an annual treatment to manage the insect. Do you treat? Do you know why the ones on the southeast have the insect? Is there another fix?

In this example, the choice of *Pieris* for the shadier, cooler side of the house was perfect. The choice is less fitting for the sunnier, hotter side of the house. Those plants are being stressed by the hot south sun, and stressed plants are easy targets for insects. Now you have a choice, you can treat the plants annually, which is easy and a forever cost, or you can decide to change out the plants, a one-time cost that requires a little more effort in the moment. Making a new plant choice is a holistic problem-solving approach for the plant and for the garden. And now, you have a great excuse to move plants around and to go plant shopping!

An example of a problem we don't have much control over are winter moths. Here in Massachusetts, we had a terrible problem with this nonnative insect that was identified as occurring locally in 2003. The moths were causing dangerous defoliation of many trees in the springtime. Treatments from sprays to predators were developed to manage this devastating insect. It was a necessary effort to save our trees. At the writing of this book, over fifteen years after the insect was identified, the pressure has started to recede, and we've been able to back off of treatments. This is a good example of appropriate research and application of treatments to respond to a new environmental pressure and to reestablish ecological balance.

Ecology

Forgive me for repeating myself, but this point is too important. If we want to be successful in our creative endeavors, we must begin by understanding that nature is made of living systems or an ecosystem, none of which operates independently of the other. The relationship between your garden and the wildlife that shares that space will evolve and change each year. Some years will be maddening with slugs, others will be amazing with butterflies. It is all good, all right, all part of the larger ecological system that ebbs and flows with each passing year.

ECOLOGY AS A SCIENCE

The term "ecology" was coined in the late nineteenth century by Ernst Haeckel, a German philosopher and professor. The term's roots are in the Greek word *oikos*, which translates as "household" or "place to live." In a nutshell, ecology is the study of the living and nonliving components of the world. It is the study of how rocks interact with other rocks, how plants interact with other plants, and how plants and rocks interact with one another. Haeckel believed in the whole with each unique piece a functioning part of the whole. He drew amazing illustrations of beautiful, intricate organisms, each organism highly unique and yet similar and all part of a fully functioning whole.

In the early twentieth century, Howard Odum expanded the idea of ecology. He said that ecology is really a system. To paraphrase him a bit, "Okay, I am going to look at the study of living and nonliving things, and I am going to overlay humans tramping around in those systems, and I am going to overlay energy." By energy, he meant the flux of energy through weather, solar energy, and the energy of the tectonic plates shifting the earth, which cause continents to drift and entire mountain ranges to rise to the heavens. All this energy is moving all the time. It is a vibration, a hum, and it is often subtle but always there. Some of these subtle forms of energy vibration will be the simple things like the feel of a soft breeze or the gentle warmth of the early morning sun. We don't think of these forms of energy as having an impact, but they do. Both create drying and warming effects that change the quality of the air by reducing the moisture. This is all good, right? Until that is all you have and then the drying, warming trend begins to compound. This is why we need variety in our weather. Gray days and rainy days do as much good as those picturesque blue-sky days.

Odum's ecology was more of an environmental ecology informed by his work with general systems theory. General systems theory was proposed in the 1940s by Ludwig von Bertalanffy, and it is built on the premise that systems are far more than the sum of their parts. If you take something apart, you have lots of things that are no longer engaged in a relationship to something else. The idea was that understanding the things or parts meant you could understand the system. Bertalanffy argued that this was not the case at all, especially with natural systems. He suggested that "things" communicate with one another and have transactions or interchanges with one another. This makes systems dynamic and changeable. Just think of it this way: families are systems, and how many families do you know that operate with full and accountable predictability based on some preconceived model?

As you read about this evolution of ecology, you may start

getting a sense of what building a Life-Scape is all about. It's looking at all of these layers within our environment and creating a vision that embraces each of them so that you are able to develop a fully functioning system.

ECOLOGY IN YOUR GARDEN

Today we have a wonderful new influx of thinkers, scientists, and designers sharing their take on ecology and living systems. Douglas W. Tallamy and Rick Darke authored the book *The Living Landscape: Designing for Beauty and Biodiversity in the Home Garden*. It is one of my favorite resources for creating beautiful gardens that nurture human beings and foster wildlife. When you start thinking about the landscape in terms of ecology and systems, it all makes sense. You can see the importance of approaching landscaping in terms of a systems-driven process or mindset, rather than the product-driven mindset of today.

Ecology in the garden is the process of blending various living and nonliving components to create an environment that includes and invites both plants and animals to participate and engage in it. An environment that is imagined and constructed by the gardener for the gardener. It is critical to accept that the act of garden making, whether for food production, floral delights, play activities, or community engagement, is a construct of the human mind reaching for beauty and function in our world. So when you are really looking at garden ecology, you overlay the gardener's imagination, your imagination.

When we throw imagination into the mix, we are moving away from the idea of completely natural. We are respecting nature. We are without a doubt working with ecosystems. But we are creating something that is not natural because gardens aren't natural in their initial inception. We make them from many elements of nature, but they are really a construct of our imagination. When we play with this idea that *we* are somehow gifted and powerful enough to do what *nature* does, we act with hubris and pride that can only get us into trouble. The goal is humility and partnership in all things gardening. Act with the knowledge that everything may change and that we are engaging in a practice of working hand in hand with nature, but that nature may have a change of heart at any moment. Eyes and hearts open to receive and respond create the best gardening experience.

The Evolving Landscape

With a Life-Scape, you are designing using natural elements and seeing if you can organize them in a way so that you might create a new ecological environment that will coexist and mature as a unit. Each element will act individually and communally within the system.

Your garden will become an ecosystem that you partner with as it moves forward because it will move forward, and you want it to. Over the course of twenty years, your landscape will evolve from new to mature to aged. Your job is to work within that evolution of growth and to respond where response is necessary to maintain the design intent and focus of your original goal.

Throughout this cycle plants will grow up, out, down, and all around. You may have thought about what they should be or will become, but they will likely get bigger than you imagined and may evolve into a shape you couldn't have imagined. You can take a chainsaw, electric hedge trimmer, and loppers and try to beat them back, but the truth is that would just be wasting your energy and damaging to your investment. A better use of your energy is to work with your changing landscape. If your instincts are telling you, "That plant is just too big for that spot now," the right response action may be transplanting it to a better location or just letting it go entirely and removing it, rather than manhandling it into conformity.

Guiding Rather than Controlling

What is it about being human that makes control such a big issue? We have the idea that we need to control or dominate nature rather than work in partnership with her. Historically, it makes sense. For centuries, we fought back the wilderness to build homes and to survive so we mistakenly think that by beating our yards into submission and slapping on quick fixes, we are making headway. Plants are living things, yet we manhandle them on a whim, rushing in to shear and chop and hack off limbs. Plants are majestic, sweet, nourishing, and hold beauty beyond compare. We should be tending, nurturing, and gently guiding plants to become the amazing, mature beings they were meant to be, possibly more majestic than they could be in the wild, absent our love and attention.

You are going to exercise some control. If you are training a hedge, then you will definitely be pruning it to shape. You need to know what the hedge needs, how far to cut back, and when to cut back. You will need to understand the plant and have the right tools before diving in. Rather than controlling by brute force, we might consider exerting control with a larger vision in mind. And sometimes, or, let's face it, all the time, that vision evolves as we live in a place longer and our lives change. In the end, the Life-Scape model suggests that we, along with our landscape vision, evolve to meet our needs and desires. You will definitely be controlling, but more along the lines of guiding or nurturing with a reasonable end-goal in mind.

Top 10 Practices to Let Go of in the Garden

1. **Trimming with hedge shears.** Unless you are making a perfect hedge out of privet or some other wildly forgiving plants, hedge shears have no place in a garden.

2. **Creating cones, balls, and squares.** These are not natural shapes for shrubs. If you are not creating a topiary garden or a sculpture park stop turning nature into geometric shapes.

3. **Spreading dyed mulch.** With few exceptions, jet black, bright red, purple, or aquamarine soil does not exist in the natural landscape, so why on earth would we choose these colors for mulch?

4. **Mulching yearly.** If you want to promote health in the garden, think about mulching every other year. In the off year you can top-dress any thin areas and just turn and fluff the mulch from the previous year.

5. **Laying weed fabric.** It does not stop weeds. It only creates a block to the natural flow of oxygen and water to the soil microbes that need it.

6. **Lining beds with rocks.** Piles and rows of little rocks on the edge of a lawn to demarcate a bed line will not reduce maintenance. It will increase it because you cannot manage the edge when there are rocks in the way.

7. **Using pebbles and rocks as mulch.** They are not mulch and they do not effectively keep weeds out. Weed seeds will edge their way in and grow wherever they can get a foothold. Rock mulch just makes it harder to weed because the soil or dirt gets mixed with the rocks and makes a mess.

8. **Weeding freehand.** It doesn't do the job. Use a tool when you weed. A cultivator, a blade, a hook, or a hoe of some kind to pull the weed from its roots will be the best way to truly get the weed out, especially perennial problem weeds with deep roots.

9. **Pruning with cheap anvil-type pruners.** These do more damage than good. When you decide to master pruning, invest in a high-quality pair of bypass pruning shears, a sharpening stone, and cleaning solution so that your pruning does only good things for the plants you tend.

10. **Trying to exert control.** It is an illusion that causes more harm than good. We don't control our gardens; we partner with them to roll with the seasons and to overcome the hurdles a natural system can throw at you. Be prepared for loss, destruction, death, and failure at every turn, then celebrate the beauty and tranquility you will witness despite the forces working against you.

THE LIFE OF TREES: GUIDANCE VERSUS CONTROL

Let's look at choosing a tree for your yard. First, you need to ask, *Why a tree?* What's the end goal? It could be for shade or to add a touch of ceiling to a space to define the upper limits of the garden. You may desire some screening from upper windows or protection from wind. Then, you choose the right place in the landscape where the addition of a tree would further this overarching goal. And *last,* you start to think about which trees might do the job in that selected space in your landscape. Tie the three items together: the need, the place, and then the tree. Keep in mind which trees are suited to your ecosystem, which will thrive with little intervention, and which will support the animals that will benefit from this new habitat in your landscape.

Select and Plant Your Tree

Next, purchase the tree making sure you pick a good specimen. This means you want the tree to meet some standard for health as well as have a strong form. For example, in a shade tree, look for a straight trunk and a nice even crown. If you are looking for an evergreen, you generally want a single and strong central trunk with an even full form. Then plant the tree using best practices. By best practices, I mean plant the tree in an appropriately sized hole, not too deep or too narrow, with the appropriate soil additives. Most new trees could use some compost, minerals, and possibly some mycorrhiza fungi added to the planting mix. Best practices also suggest that mulching, watering, and staking might be appropriate for the needs of the tree as well as the location. Now, with all that planning and initial best practices behind you, all you have left is to make sure your tree gets adequate hydration for the next year. Monitor for any pests or diseases, of course, and treat as needed, but otherwise leave the tree to acclimate and settle in.

Nurture Your Tree to Maturity

In years two through ten, you will guide that tree's growth

by pruning. If it is an evergreen, it will need far less attention, unless you are growing and training a hedge. For your new shade or ornamental tree, avoid stripping the insides, topping it, or shearing it. Simply watch the scaffolding of the branches and the architecture and the overall shape. You may take out a couple branches here and there to guard against crossing and crowding. Make sure there is a really strong structure and branching throughout the canopy and that there are no areas where the tree branches grow so close together that they fuse, which can cause areas of weakness over time. Make sure there is only one dominant leader, which is the stem that is driving the tree upward, and watch for competition from co-dominant stems. (If you'd like to learn more about pruning, I suggest picking up *The Pruning Book: Completely Revised and Updated* by Lee Reich.) When you follow these practices over time, your tree is going to grow with a beautiful structure. The scaffolding will be resilient enough to handle snow and it will become the umbrella you want to shade that deck on the south side of your house.

<u>Leave it Alone</u>

After ten years, you will ideally no longer need to touch the tree. You basically leave it alone, and let that tree be what it is going to be. If you planted and placed it well, there will likely be little need to toy with it unless it becomes damaged. With older trees that we inherit when we purchase a property, they may just keep getting bigger and bigger and we need to accommodate them as they grow—especially if they are specimens we love. It's also a fact that trees mature out and start to decline in time, in which case more proactive care to keep a tree alive longer or to mitigate hazards will be necessary.

OWNERSHIP VERSUS STEWARDSHIP

Following this model, you are managing, nurturing, and guiding. You are a steward of your tree rather than an owner. Take a look at the juxtaposition of these two words: ownership versus stewardship. *Ownership* suggests that we have exclusive rights to something. Stewardship suggests that we have a responsibility for it. Ownership would say we have control. Stewardship would say we are obligated to nurture. Ownership implies possession while stewardship implies partnership. The ownership mindset is very dominating and controlling, and the stewardship mindset is very protecting and caretaking. With a Life-Scape, we shift from an ownership mentality to a stewardship mentality, which we will cover in much more detail in part four of the book.

You have an agenda with your landscape, trees, and hedges that can be considered control or design intent, but it doesn't involve wielding hedge shears or hacking away, forcing the plants into submission. You are not saying "Stay, stay, stay, stay, stay" to the same plants, so that they never change. Instead, you are saying, "Grow this way, be this shape, be this height and width, because I want you to fit nicely in this space."

You are helping the plant to be itself but in the context of what you want it to be within your garden or landscape. Your desires and those of the plants are not mutually exclusive. They have to meld and form into some unity. Since the plant isn't able to make decisions and changes in its form, it is up to you to intuit what the plant will allow in the way of guidance so that together you find harmony. Your intuition is informed by what you research about the tree, both in books and from examples in nature, combined with your feelings and assumptions about this tree and its presence on your property.

***

Connecting your feelings about your home with the purpose of all plants and elements of your landscape is, in fact, the core essence of the Life-Scape model—from imagining your dream to designing and building to living and evolving with your landscape for years to come.

 # TODAY'S TASKS

1. Think about the systems thinking approach and ask yourself how your project can align with the systems presenting themselves in your landscape.

2. Notice the nature around your home now. What's there? How would you characterize your landscape? Hot and dry, shaded and moist, windy and exposed?

3. Make a list of plants you have—the trees, shrubs, and perennials—in your landscape now. Note the ones you like and the ones that look healthy. List the ones you don't like and the ones that look like they are struggling or sick or have bug issues.

THE FIRST THREE STEPS TO ACHIEVING SUCCESS IN YOUR LIFE-SCAPE

"A clear vision, backed by definite plans, gives you a tremendous feeling of confidence and personal power."

—Brian Tracy, *The Gifts of Self-Confidence*

Before you start the work of planning, building, and maintaining your landscape, it's a good idea to get very clear about the scope of your project and the investment.

You will need to:

- Identify your reasons for embarking on your landscape project in the first place.

- Determine your key players in the development process.

- Define your site, which includes your garden setting and your style.

Identify Your Reasons

To really understand what you want from your landscape,

you have to dig down into your deepest need. For anything we crave, we have an underlying need or desire that pushes us. For a landscape it isn't *just* about the plants. Start by asking yourself, *What is the underlying driver for creating my landscape in the first place?* Maybe you want to elevate your status in your neighborhood, or with family, friends, or work colleagues. There is nothing wrong with that. Maybe you are looking for an escape, a creative and physical outlet to get away from your mind chatter, your worries from work, kids, or just life. Or you might want a place to rest, a secluded and safe area to recharge. Perhaps you simply love being outside and want to live out there in comfort with friends and family on as many occasions as possible.

Your need will inform every phase of your project. It is a point you will come back to again and again to truly create your Life-Scape, making sure each step aligns with your driving desire. The point here is that whether you DIY or partner with professionals, this is an inside job. It is first and foremost about creating your version of outdoor living at home. And that is personal!

Your core desire or need for this work in your yard will be the driving force for all your decision-making. Let's use the scenario of loving to entertain outside. The decisions you make about your Life-Scape plan will have to go back to this core desire. For example, when choosing trees, consider their size at maturity and whether the eventual change to the amount of sun exposure as the tree matures will put a damper on your enjoyment of that space. Or is your goal to add the shade for comfort and coolness? Every choice you make will go back to this central desire if you just ask the question, "How does this plant, patio, fence get me closer to my ultimate goal?"

Determine Key Players in the Development Process

After you determine your need and before you even begin dreaming and imagining your Life-Scape, which I discuss in chapter 4, you need to determine who's going to do the work. Consider how much, if any, you are willing to do or can do, and how much work you want to put in the hands of professionals.

YOUR ROLE—SELECT YOUR AVATAR

Throughout my career in the landscaping industry I've noticed that homeowners fall into three major types, in terms of the mindset they bring to home-improvement projects. These types, which I call the Actor, the Director, and the Audience, are gradients on a continuum. You can lean toward one type, yet have attributes of another.

I refer to these avatars throughout the book. Before going further, see if you can identify your avatar by reading through the avatar list in the sidebar. You may find you share traits of two types—an Actor/Director or an Audience/Director, for example—which is fine. Once you identify your avatar, you will be able to determine the role you want to play in your landscaping project and the partners you will need.

Who Are You?

- **Actor.** The hands-on creator/builder of this project. The act of doing is necessary for you. Your question is, *Are you the lead or a supporting member of the cast?*

- **Director.** The one in charge of this project. The act of managing and oversight is important to you. Your question is, *Are you an active project manager type, or more of the stand-back CEO type?*

- **Audience.** This project will be accomplished through the active engagement of others. The act of observing progress is meaningful to you. The most important question that you must answer for yourself is, *How do you develop a comfortable trust relationship so that you can be hands off?*

Actor

If you are an Actor, you are interested in getting your hands dirty at some point during this process. That could mean actively participating in selecting design or materials. You may want to be the one to demolish an existing deck or the tree fort your kids have outgrown. Creating the project workflow might be interesting to you, and you may enjoy being the one to buy the materials. You may be the one who will build the hardscape feature or plant the shrubs and perennials. You may even want to take care of this landscape.

While you might have the financial means to play the role of Director for your project, you believe in your core that you can do the work. In fact, you may absolutely love to do the work and have a long history of completing hands-on projects.

Actors may still find reasons to partner with a professional, even if they have earlier successes behind them. Maybe you have done a lot of the work on this project already and decide to call in some help because of a turning point that changes your outlook or ability. A turning point might be:

- **You have injured yourself or damaged your property.** Now you want to determine how much of the project you are going to hand over while you heal. If you damaged something during the project, you may be ready for a pro to help you out of a jam.

- **The project is just taking up too much of your time:.** You may decide to hire someone to oversee the rest of the project, while remaining engaged in some of the action steps of the work. Perhaps you need someone who specializes in sprinkler systems or tree care or masonry to take on those unique parts of the job for you.

- **You suffered just one too many failures and complications.** To alleviate burnout, you might decide to partner with someone who can explain the big picture to you, and then the two of you can discuss the areas where your efforts will be the most valuable. Together, you will map out fixes and the task flow.

No matter why you are calling in a service provider or what kind of help you need, you want to be very clear with yourself about what might be too heavy to lift, too complicated to finish, or pose the biggest risk for property damage or personal injury.

The point is that you want to *do* part of this project on some level. The question for you is, *Are you the lead or a supporting member of the cast?*

Director

You may have the budget to be an Audience but the overall process is very important to you. You want to understand the flow; what comes first, second, third, and so on. You may even want to take on some token part of the work yourself for the sheer enjoyment of involving yourself in the unfolding of the project. You may like the idea of saving a little by investing a little sweat equity in the project. Whether you take on active work or not, you are someone who needs to understand the big picture, all the moving parts, how they work together, and how you fit in.

You will be happiest in a partnership where you can offer ideas and direction, where you will be heard. You want to partner with professionals who are willing to keep you in the loop at all times, who ask for and welcome your input and critique of the work at regular intervals. Partner with someone who enjoys and realizes the value of collaborating with you. All these points can be negotiated before you sign the contract.

The question to ask yourself is, *Are you a hands-on Director, or directing from a distance?*

Audience

If you are this type of homeowner, you have the budget and the mindset to employ service providers to get the work done for you. You may not be uber wealthy, but you have enough disposable income to enlist the help of professionals in the design development, implementation, and management of your home. You are interested in the aesthetic, but the process?

Not so much. You are definitely interested in the outcome, and the overall feel of your new space, but you don't want to do any of the work yourself nor do you have the need to be overly informed about the step by step details of the process.

You want to find a service provider who gets you. Someone who knows how to draw out your desires and translates the bits and pieces of what you say into designs, actions, and outcomes that delight you. You want to trust this professional to follow through with your best interest and your project success in mind.

Ask yourself, *Are you most comfortable handing this off to a trusted team?*

BE HONEST ABOUT YOUR ROLE

For the Audience type it's easy to be honest with yourself. This group is often crystal clear that they don't want to do any of the work. For the Director and Actor types, it can be a little trickier. So here's a tip:

When you choose your role, please remember to avoid the assumption that any project is totally straightforward. Let's take installing a new section of lawn. Super simple, right? You can just toss on some seed or roll out some sod, mow when it grows, fertilize as the bag recommends, and be good to go. Nope. Actually, lawn projects can be complex at times.

Whether you want a plain ordinary lawn or an organic lawn, they require a certain level of attention to the details before getting it just right. Plan to study enough to get an overview of what the project entails, then decide whether you are going to dive in and learn how to do the job, partner with somebody, or completely hand it off to an expert.

I often have my clients who are Directors and Actors fill out a list of tasks and follow these steps:

1. Rate each task: I love this. I am okay with this. I hate this. Everything you hate, you will pass off to a service provider.

2. Then come back to the tasks you love and those you are okay with and rate those: I can do this. I cannot do this. Add the cannot dos to the list of the tasks you will hand off.

3. Then come back to the tasks you love and that you can do, and take another pass, answering with: I will do this. I may do this. I probably won't do this. Hand off the tasks you probably won't do.

Just because you *can do* a task, doesn't mean you *will do* it. In fact, these *can-do* items are often the jobs that don't get done because you know you can do them, but ultimately you don't because you are just too busy with everything you have on your plate already. Similarly, the items you *may do* often hit the bottom of the list because you just get busy or distracted. It may be wise to hand off those questionable tasks as well. In gardening, you want to stick with only the things you love and know for certain that you will do, because they will get done even when you are busy and distracted. You are committed. Everything else should be outsourced. The garden waits for no one.

FINDING GARDEN PARTNERS: WHO IS OUT THERE TO HELP YOU

The development of a trade skill or creative skill is neither quick nor easy. The process of building anything, whether it is a garden, a house, or a bridge, requires amassing a set of skills. Those skills must be developed through practice, dedication, and a whole lot of trial and error— hopefully light on the error, for everyone's sake. Of course, a lot more leniency is possible when there is error in a garden because error in a house or a bridge can spell disaster! It is important to honor the process of developing any trade skill that inherently has a creative edge to it. Dedicated tradespeople are a unique set of crafty professionals who understand the rules and know how to problem-solve.

In the following section, I have broken down the development of a professional tradesperson into three levels or stages. I'm using the term "tradesperson" to refer to professionals in the field of gardening, landscaping, designing, or building a landscape. While these trades are often presented separately in the marketplace, it is important to (a) unify these creative building skills, and (b) address the stages as it pertains to the entire trade, not just one slice of it.

The Producer Stage

This is the period of development when a tradesperson learns the order of things, when to do tasks within a hierarchical thinking model. For example, at the producer stage a gardener might approach a lawn this way: If the grass is growing, cut it. Now the lawn is shorter, so mission accomplished. Or if the lawn needs to be greener, fertilize it. It is green now so that means success.

In the producer stage, the tradesperson isn't overly concerned with the underlying details of why tasks are completed or not. They aren't really asking why, *Why is the grass growing so much, or why is it getting dull and yellow?* The work at this stage of professional skill development is almost completely outcome or results driven. With our grass example, the answer to *Why mow it?* is simple. *It's Tuesday, and the lawn hasn't been mowed since last Tuesday.* It's time to mow. For the producer stage tradesperson, all landscaping and gardening tasks can be simplified into a timetable or a production timeline, so that they are done in some predictable order which helps in communicating with their clientele.

You might hire a tradesperson at the producer stage to cut your lawn, weed your beds, rake the fall leaves, or maybe to plow and shovel snow. You would not hire a producer stage tradesperson to prune your coveted Japanese maple, design your arrival experience at the front of your home, or even install a new patio in your backyard.

The reason? Because this person is a garden handyman with a basic understanding of the immediate cause and effect of an action. This person is not going to be up on the codes or best practices that govern those actions, such as the building codes for hardscape features, horticultural codes that guide decision-making when choosing and managing plants, or environmental codes that may direct onsite actions toward conservation or sustainability.

To be clear, there is nothing wrong with the producer stage tradesperson; they are valuable assets in project development and in maintenance. Within this stage there are varying degrees of skill that come with specialization and years in the business.

The Method Stage

This period of development usually comes after the producer stage, but the stages can overlap. The tradesperson at the method stage is still concerned with the hierarchy of tasks and subsequent results but now also has some information about the rules and best practices that govern the work. In this stage they often begin to focus on a specific gardening element, landscape style, or building technique. Think of the method stage as the time when the tradesperson's interest is piqued by a particular method of their craft. For example, a gardener may take up a broad topic like organic gardening or a more focused topic like vegetable gardening. Or maybe it is a particular area of expertise, such as native landscapes or ornamental grasses. A landscape contractor may become interested in developing patio spaces, ponds, or building walls, while another may become more focused on tree care and pursue arboriculture.

You might hire a tradesperson at the method stage to prune that coveted Japanese maple because they are a collector of maples and a certified arborist. You hire a landscape contractor to build you a new patio because they are certified by the International Concrete Paving Institute (ICPI). They love the art of setting pavers and are up on all the latest techniques. Or you hire a gardener to build you an organic vegetable garden because they have become an Accredited Organic Land Care Provider (AOLCP) and specialize in growing heirloom plants.

The Mastery Stage

Tradespeople in this period of development have mastered the producer stage and immersed themselves in numerous methods, styles, and techniques, so have passed through the method stage. Most have been in the business at least 15 years.

The tradesperson at this level begins to see the garden as more than just something to do, build, or manage. At this stage, they realize that gardens and humans are inextricably linked and that all the skills meld into one purpose that requires that they are designed, built, and managed in unity. The clarity around that unity begins to drive design ideas, including the notion that sustainability and conservation are central to success and satisfaction. There is a level of humility that enters the mindset of the tradesperson at this stage because the vastness of the art and science has now come to light. They have been doing it long enough to look back, see where they may have gone wrong, and learn from those mistakes.

You might hire a someone at this level to help repair or develop a comfortable outside environment while honoring the surrounding trees or wetlands. This tradesperson can assist in bringing an old landscape back from being neglected while honoring the original design intent. They will identify the best plant palette and materials or help you imagine and develop a landscape that will weave in all the current and future needs of your family while adding to the value of your property.

Mastery stage professionals are often very well connected in the industry. They will have select partner contractors in various concentrations of the method stage of development who are honing their skills in a narrow focus to become an expert. These trade partners make up a dynamic resource that the mastery stage tradesperson will utilize in your project development.

MATCHMAKING

The trick now is to match the tradesperson with your personality type. There are various combinations that may work well for any given project. The trick is to get clear about who you are as a homeowner *and* maybe as a gardener, too, then make a good match with a well-aligned tradesperson. If you are building a Japanese-style garden, you really don't need someone who is at the mastery stage; you need somebody who is steeped in this style of garden making and tending.

If you are a total down and dirty do-it-yourselfer all you may need is a great guy with a backhoe. You need a partner with the muscle and proper insurances to do what you aren't able to do yourself. If you work hard and stick with your producer stage partner, you will be fine and may have some fun too.

There are many Actor and Director types who would love to work with tradespeople at the mastery stage in a consulting relationship. I do a lot of that type of partnering, and it is super-fun on both sides. When I am working with a DIY person, I have a blast feeding them useful information, sharing insider tips, and batting around fun design ideas. They get excited to get to work, and then I leave them to it. The trick is to know who *you* are, know who *they* are, and find your match.

As with any team, the players, how they play, and what their core values and goals are will determine your success. Yes, it takes time to assemble the right players. But if you are planning on spending money to develop a landscape, or better yet, a Life-Scape, then you want to pace yourself so that you make the most of the investment. Any capital investment in your outside living environment will need long-term care considerations— meaning how you build it will be the foundation for how you care for it. (More about that in chapters 7 and 8.) Remember, not all projects are the same. There is no one-size-fits-all solution or team. Thoughtful creation of your team will result in the best outcome and experience.

Define Your Garden Setting

You can think of the garden setting as the stage upon which you will choreograph the masterpiece, which is your homestead. We don't use that word much anymore, but it is a good way to describe what your land and home represent. The beginning of this journey should be when you first start looking for your home, but the reality is that there is so much to think about when selecting a home that the landscape is often pretty far down on the list, if it's even on the list. Most people start thinking about their landscape well after they've purchased their home, sometimes many years after.

At that point, it's time to develop your Big Ultimate Dream (BUD) for what your home will feel like and represent to you. I love this acronym because a bud of any flower holds all the potential for what will be in the future. It is an unfinished idea cued up to develop when the conditions are right and bloom at the perfect time. And even the action of blooming isn't all at once, it is an unfolding that happens in timed sequence. The reality is that most people do not have this information before they embark on homeownership. That doesn't mean that you shouldn't do the exercise now, right where you are. And keep in mind that a BUD that is in alignment with where you are now is the most attainable.

As you get started, avoid the one critical mistake of dreaming up a setting or outcome that is conflicts with your current setting. One example of that is envisioning a large, flat lawn with a lovely pool and cabana when you live in a home that is set on sloped, wooded land filled with ledge stone throughout the soil. It isn't to say you *can't* have what you want, but you can be sure it will be a great deal of work and a lot of money to get it. Another example is dreaming of a sunny, open landscape when your home is nestled in a tree-filled landscape that has water running through the woods. This may be a jurisdictional property regulated by the Department of Environmental Protection and a strict wetland bylaw. No manner of wanting or money will get you what you want in this case. If you find yourself in a setting that you don't like, be realistic about what you can be chang easily versus what will take time, effort, and a big investment to change.

Step one is to get crystal clear about what you own and what your land is all about. You *have* to know your site! I can't stress this enough. The top three natural resources you need to assess and understand on your personal plot are soil, water, and sun. You should also understand the land around you and your community. These are the building blocks for an ecosystem. Understand what is available to you on and around your property, now. I will go into more detail about site analysis in chapter 5, but I wanted to introduce you to this concept early in the process.

WHAT IS YOUR STYLE?

Style is as important in garden making as it is in building your wardrobe. Your style says something about you, but it also has the power to create comfort and a sense of ease that you want in your life.

If you focus on all the details of gardening you will find many styles to choose from such as English, cottage, Japanese, traditional, Mediterranean, country, Tuscan, and more. To help focus on the basics, I whittled down a very long list to three main garden types that will help you determine your style, noted in the sidebar.

Three Main Garden Constructs

- **Formal** — highly patterned and organized in a very discernable way, often symmetrical and always balanced

- **Informal** — loose organization (but still organized); allows some randomness and breaks from symmetry and balance

- **Thematic** — gravitates to a theme that drives the aesthetic, like a Japanese-style garden, a white garden, or a water garden

These three styles can be blended and all of them may be present in a landscape, but usually there is an underlying style that is carried out in any landscape. For example, if you are drawn to a formal style, then you may be very formal at the front of the house, loosen up a little in the back, and then loosen up a little more along the edges. This formality, organization, repetition, balance, and symmetry are carried out through the entire landscape.

WHAT IS YOUR PALETTE?

Here's the good news—you don't have to worry about matching colors in your garden. Why? Flowers don't clash; it doesn't work that way in nature. Colors do communicate feelings, like boldness or softness. Ask yourself if you want the color volume turned up to be bolder (hot colors, jewel tones) or turned down to be softer (paler colors, pastel tones). You can go for more symmetrical and balanced colors—staying on one side of the color wheel, like varying shades of pinks—or you can add in a color from the other side to complement, like a yellow for pop. The other version is to put in a riot of color—that means basically using all the colors at once—because sometimes a riot is fun. Or you can go with a more monochromatic look, such as all white backed up with varying tones of green.

Just because you choose one color preference doesn't mean you have to stick with it throughout your landscape. You may love the soft, soothing effect of a white garden and want that in a shaded corner with a bench and a short stone path leading to it from a more open lawn space. Beyond that on the other side of the property, you may decide that loads of color is exactly what you want to see in the sunny area. Remember, you are creating rooms. Like rooms in your house, you can paint those rooms with different colors and use different fabrics to offer a change in texture. These same design principles translate into the making of your landscape.

***

By this point, you should feel very clear about who you are as a landscape owner, what you need in a service provider, and the *feel* of what you want to create aesthetically. Remember, the whole purpose is to help you line up the work in a way that will be calm and productive for you. The goal is to help you to focus in on what you really love and enjoy so that what you build is in alignment with who you are.

TODAY'S TASKS

1. Identify the core driver that is pushing you forward to plan this landscape project.

2. Determine your avatar type: Actor, Director, Audience. Be honest with yourself.

3. Think about what stage of tradesperson you'd like to work with - Producer, Method, Master. Maybe research companies in your area.

4. Start outlining your Big Ultimate Dream (BUD) - your setting and your style. Maybe start looking around your neighborhood more to get a feel for what's around you.

PART II

GETTING STARTED

My goal for Part II is to teach you how to activate your creativity and realize that you can create an environment based on your desires and dreams. In Part II, you will learn how to tap into your dreams and refine them by envisioning and defining each space, like driveway, deck, pool, and so on, by experience. You'll think about arrival, social, transitional, and forgotten spaces. You will collect data for sun, soil, and water conditions so the plants that you choose will thrive in your new Life-Scape. At the end of Part II, I hope you will realize your own innate creativity, feel a deepening affinity for your land, and see possibilities where you might have previously seen limitations. Then in Part III, I will provide you with the tools to help you understand the potential for making those dreams come true with your current homestead.

DARE TO DREAM

"Without leaps of imagination or dreaming, we lose the excitement of possibilities. Dreaming, after all is a form of planning."

—Gloria Steinem

Developing your vision is the backbone of design. Before we can design our finished product, we need to see the image of the final outcome in our imagination. It just makes sense. If you dive into technical drawing or start digging and planting right away, you will waste precious effort and resources. You as the homeowner must be the one to jumpstart the effort with your dreams. You need to start with *your* vision. What do you want? Where is your emotional wisdom pulling you? A dream or vision captures your feelings and desires which are the absolute center of your Life-Scape. You are not only designing a space, you are imagining what you will do in that space. You are imagining the memories you will create, the problems you will solve, and the rest and relaxation you will have in this new space. You are bringing all the pieces together that will create the WOW factor.

The wow factor is personal. It isn't based on keeping up

with the Joneses. After all, why would you plant the same blue hydrangeas in your front yard that all your neighbors have planted if you hate blue? Maybe you prefer a soft white selection or another shrub altogether. Sure, there are rules of design and you can consult books for more information about those. This chapter is about finding what works for you. A Life-Scape is personal. It is about you, your family, your life, and the current *stage* of your life. To get the wow, you want to incorporate things that are awe inspiring to you like the color, texture, fragrance, sound, and compositions that make your heart sing.

When you begin tapping into your dream and creating your vision, you are activating the right side of your brain, which is the creative, spatial side. If you get caught up in the "how to," you will stymie the entire exercise because you will be entering back into the more analytical side of the brain. In Betty Edwards's book *Drawing on the Right Side of the Brain*, she says, "The drawing isn't all that hard . . . Seeing is the problem." For our purposes, we can substitute the word "designing" for "drawing." And the daring to dream phase is all about helping you to see.

You know the saying "A picture is worth 1,000 words"? When it comes to design, a dream or a vision is worth 1,000 design plans. I would like you to envision the whole before the parts. Develop the big picture with your creative right brain.

Then we will cover the next steps of engaging with your left brain to take your vision apart and figure out how to build it. Of course, I can write all I want to about visioning, but I am relying on words. I write and you decode, which are all left-brain activities. But stick with me because I am going to share a few of the tools I use to help my clients formulate their vision. Together we will get there.

Capturing Your Big Ultimate Dream

When I first begin working with my clients, I ask them to capture their BUD. Your Big Ultimate Dream may feel huge and unattainable, but it is real and jam-packed with potential. While this may sound all woo-woo and weird, the free-association process taught by the artist Craig Smallish is a great way to tap into the feelings and desires that will become the basis for your dream and vision. Free association is most commonly credited to Sigmund Freud. Picture yourself in psychoanalysis, lying on a comfy couch talking about your dream garden. You just say whatever comes to mind, with no concern about the coherence, validity, or appropriateness of what comes up. You just speak your thoughts, ideas, and desires. Again, this may seem like a departure from some of the factual data I've shared so far, but the goal is to free your mind of its inner-censor so you can allow what is buried to come to the surface. In a nutshell, Craig Smallish retrofit this technique to fit the creative process. He says that you start by jotting down simple characteristics, values, or traits of the thing you are exploring. Don't think about it; just let words flow. One word spontaneously sparks the next thought. The goal is to land in the realm of uncharted thoughts and ideas that will allow you to get closer to the true nature of your desire. It is simple but requires focus. If you want more information about the free-association process, you can search online for "Craig Smallish free-association process" to find articles and even a free course!

Envisioning Your Space

Next, you will tap into an inner feeling for the space and solution to determine the best way to start designing. In our modern lives, we all move so fast that we rarely tap into our feelings in this way. Visions are usually blurry at first. The best way to do this dreaming is to be in the space that is inspiring you or the place that is troubling you. You have to actually go to the place in question or make sure you are viewing it so that you can tap into the inner wisdom that will guide your visioning.

Here is an example of how this exercise might work. Imagine you are out in the landscape of the new house you just bought. You start thinking about how you are going to live in this new home and on this new land. Let's say you are eager to have a veggie garden and maybe grow some herbs. You find yourself wandering over to the sunniest part of the yard. You turn your face up to the sun and drink in some Vitamin D, and in that moment, you start to imagine tomatoes and basil, carrots, and maybe a run of asparagus. Then you think, *It would be great to have a little tool shed and compost bins right near the garden and easy access to water.* As you are dreaming, you notice you are smiling. You open your eyes and, in that moment, you see exactly where the shed will be. You see where you will place your compost bins. You get a fleeting thought of berries and start to imagine a berry patch lining the north side of the veggie plot. You feel satisfied with your dream and wonder, *Now, how do I make this dream real?*

Defining Your Spaces

The previous exercise focuses on one space rather than the entire landscape. Breaking down your outdoor living experience into spaces such as rooms, then feeling and seeing each distinct space (or "room"), makes creating your vision much more manageable. You may be thinking, *What are the spaces inside a landscape?* I like to break each down by considering the experiences within those spaces or rooms.

ARRIVAL EXPERIENCE

This experience includes all the public spaces in your landscape. If your house is exposed to the road, the public space is the entire visible front. If it is set back and out of sight, the public spaces are the separate pieces experienced one by one as you travel to the home. Your arrival experience is the first impression, so you want it to be a welcoming one. This is what realtors call "curb appeal."

Key Points of the Arrival Experience

- **Parking areas.** Make sure the areas where you and your guests park are comfortable and easy to navigate. Avoid making visitors nervous with the parking situation.

- **Main entries to the house.** Determine which will be the main entry for your family. Then decide if you want your guests to use that same entry or another one. Ideally, you will be able to see these entrances from the parking area or driveway.

- **Access or egress elements.** Determine if the walks and footpaths are wide enough for two people to walk side by side. The door for guests (the main door) should be the widest and easiest to navigate.

- **The steps, landings, stoops, porches, and doors.** Access to and use of these elements must make sense, and be comfortable and attractive. A doorway that is wide and covered is ideal for waiting comfortably in all weather.

SOCIAL SPACE

Next, think about the outdoor living experience. It is often in the backyard, but it can be in the front. There is nothing more fun than when you have an opportunity to create active space from what might otherwise be a passive space. Maybe you put in a front courtyard with benches, a tea table, and comfortable chairs. Or you mount a basketball hoop onto your garage so you can host a friendly family game of hoops. After all, the front of your home has its own charm. Why not use it?

Homeowners commonly look to their backyards as the place to hang out and develop as a living space. You want to break up that living space into parts that reflect their uses.

Social Spaces by Use

- **Playing** — a swing set, sport court, bocce court, hot tub, swimming pool

- **Cooking** — an outdoor kitchen or grill, pizza oven, smoker

- **Dining** — table and chairs for your family and to entertain guests

- **Gardening** — the shed for gardening tools and supplies, compost bin

- **Resting** — a meditation garden or an area with comfortable chairs or lounges

Within each of these sections, decide how much that space will be developed and programmed. Is your sport court going to be used for more than basketball? Do you want a moveable fire pit on your patio to permit the patio room to become convertible to other uses? These details are up to you.

TRANSITIONAL SPACES

The areas we pass through to get from one space to another are termed "transitional spaces." Often these are the areas on the sides of the house where we move from the front yard to the back. It is important that they are developed enough to make transitioning pleasurable, or you can shift them from useless to useful by giving them a purpose, such as areas for storage and utility, pets, and additional parking.

LEFTOVER OR FORGOTTEN SPACES

These are often larger transitional spaces that have not been made beautiful or useful. In the case of a funky-shaped lot, these spaces can be an odd corner of frontage or a wedge in a back corner of the property. Or they can be a leftover or forgotten space that is on the side of a new addition that is somehow cut off from the main yard spaces. These leftover or forgotten spaces can sometimes become mini jewels. When they are developed into a secluded patio, a meditation garden, or a culinary garden, they instantly become favored gems of the landscape.

Seeing Solutions

Now that you know the spaces and their elements, take the time to focus your attention on each space. You must make time to sit in that space. Be in that space. Focus on the function of that space and how it fulfills its function and how it flows. If there are any hiccups or outright problems, continue to sit in that space and open your creative mind to solutions. Trust that the answer is within you. I guarantee that good design comes from knowing the space, uncovering your desire, and then finding the alignment between the two.

VIEWS

Let's say you have a problem you want to solve with your new landscape. For instance, your next-door neighbors don't keep up their landscape. Not only does their yard look like a shabby mess, their house is not in the best shape either. You could slap up a fence between your properties but no other house on your street has a fence dividing adjacent properties. While it is within your right to have a fence if you want one, it doesn't seem right. What do you do?

1. Start by focusing your attention on the views from inside your house to the offending landscape. Which windows have the strongest views? What are you looking at? What don't you like about it?

2. Sit facing the view that makes you unhappy, close your eyes, and take a deep breath. Let the air out slowly and imagine a view out that window that would please you. And don't say the ocean or mountains, because I don't know how to build either of those. Maybe it would be nice to see some green, or a few flowers, or a statue, or a trellis with growing vines. You don't have to be fancy, just imaginative. And do not get hung up by the fact that you do not know what plants would work there; those details are not relevant in the dreaming stage.

3. Do this for each window with an offending view. Don't forget the upstairs. Sometimes the offending view is when you are looking down.

See how easy that is? You just have to dare to dream and to see that dream as a way to collect raw data for the design process. In this example, raw data is defining the problem and imagining the solution. You can collect this raw data in a journal or a sketch pad. Simply write down what you envisioned such as the colors, shapes, and heights. Remember, you are not designing at this point, you are just logging information about a vision, like trying to write down a dream you woke up remembering. A bit later in the chapter, we will talk about developing your dream by creating a vision board.

ACCESS AND FLOW

How you get to a place is a critical part of arrival because it sets up the state of mind you are in when you arrive. This is almost more important than the place itself. Why? Because you are setting the mood for how you will feel when you arrive.

Did you ever have a great party to go to and found yourself stuck in nasty traffic on the way? Put yourself back in that place for a minute. What happened to you? You have this great place to go to, all your friends will be there, and you are stuck in traffic. You get antsy, then frustrated, then annoyed, and then angry. By the time you get to the party you need two glasses of wine just to get out of your grumpy mood. Then you cannot seem to forget the horrible travel experience, so you relive it with every new person you encounter. Hmmm, how great is that party now?

Access and flow are a huge part of your experience, so you want to consider those aspects when you are in the dreaming phase. A few years ago, a new client called me because they wanted to put in a pool and needed someone to design their small backyard to accommodate it. We were sitting at their kitchen table talking about the project, when I realized how awkward it would be to get to the pool from the house.

"Okay," I said to them, "to get to the pool and patio, you have to go through the kitchen, through the dining area, into the living room, and out the French doors. That is not great. And what are you going to do with the wet kids when they come in from the pool?"

The flow just didn't make sense to me. I suggested that if it were my house, I would replace the French doors with windows and tear out the kitchen window to put in a door that opened onto a beautiful little stoop. "The flow in and out will be killer."

They loved the idea. We connected with a builder and they made the changes which solved the problem. There is no way that a pool company would have foreseen that problem. A pool company would have just seen the pool. But because we were looking at the entire project, we incorporated the house, the egress, the circulation, the pool, a patio, and a cabana. We envisioned this incredible pool oasis in their backyard. You can check out images of this project in the portfolio section on my website, *www.TheGardenContinuum.com*, under *Poolside Paradise.*

The most important part of any design is the process of arrival. Start by imagining how it feels to you when you walk around your landscape. Or, in the case of my clients, getting to and from the pool. If your first response is, "It's clunky" or "It's horrible" or "It's totally awkward," then start to identify what is bad about it. Remember that you don't need fancy design language for this process. "I hate my backyard!" works in this step of design.

Choosing Your Settings—Location, Location, Location

We just talked about arrival and the importance of setting up a good flow as you transition from one space to the next. The two main experiences of any place are the arrival experience and the rest experience. When I say "rest," I mean that once you arrive at this location you will want to stay there to play or maybe sip your coffee or entertain friends. In my previous example of the back door and the pool, the destination is the pool with a large surrounding pool deck and patio. That may be where you want to rest or hang out as the kids are playing. Why would you build a destination point you merely pass through?

Let's talk about this destination. You know that realtors say the three most important elements in buying or selling a house are location, location, location. You can say the same for siting any landscape element. Location is *key*. Your destination has to be inviting, it has to be comfortable, and it has to be functional. Let's focus more on the element of a patio.

Almost all patios are in the back of a house for a number of reasons. First up: privacy. If you are going to lounge or dine outside, you probably do not want to be on display. But what if the back of your house is not the most private? Or if your kitchen access to the outdoors is on the side of the house? And what about flow and the invitation and ease of getting to the patio from the kitchen? Maybe you have a deck off the kitchen and prefer to have a patio off your living room.

I am suggesting that you avoid a knee-jerk design solution that you think you are supposed to make just because it is what your neighbor has or what you remember from your childhood. Sometimes there is a better solution waiting for your imagination to grasp it.

For patios, we want to consider sun and shade. Too much sun and you might bake. Too much shade and you may be too chilly for comfort. A protected spot with intermittent or dappled light is generally best. You also want protection from the wind so that sitting is comfortable, and you do not lose napkins down the driveway when a gust of wind blows through.

Ideally, you want your patio on a level space—*of course the patio is level*—but crafting enough level space around the patio will be critical to make it feel connected to the house and land. Promontories (elevated spaces that give you a high-view vantage point) are nice when they feel visually well tethered to the landscape. Head back to my website and check out the *Backyard Oasis* portfolio page for a majestic promontory patio and fire pit set up.

You may find that the patio you are dreaming of would be far better situated on the side of your house with well-chosen lounge furniture that invites you to move the party outside or just comfortably escape the house with a book. You could add a door to your living room that invites you to enjoy the beautiful views of this space and that gives you access that does not involve the kitchen and dining areas. Being on the side of your property, this space could easily be connected with walks, steps, or stepping stones to the back yard and to the front garden. It may not be conventional, but it may be just the comfortable solution you were looking for. To see a fun example, go to the portfolio page called *Side Yard Patio Escape* at *www.TheGardenContinuum.com*.

Location has a lot to do with energy. By energy, I mean the vibrations of the earth and surrounding vegetation and life that may be in an area. Allow yourself to spend time in your landscape before you design anything. Knowing you want a patio is a good first step, but it is not enough. See if you can get a feeling for where it should go. Grab some light, comfortable chairs, and a cup of tea. Move yourself around the property for an hour while you enjoy your tea. Sit in each place for at least ten minutes. How do you feel in each location? Is one place remarkably better or worse than the other? Don't worry about why that is; just rank the spaces, putting your favorite spot as number one and so on down until you get to the worst space. This exercise will help you to discover the best possible location for your patio.

Creating a Vision Board

Now that you considered your space and are seeing the details, you can start a vision board. This very simple tool helps you exercise your dream muscles. A simple bulletin board works best to provide you with an easy surface to move things around. Your vision board needs to live in a place where you will see it often because it needs to be a living representation of your vision. The best location is where you will see the board and your outside space together, such as on a wall near a window or sliding glass door that looks out to the yard space you want to develop. Don't worry if you cannot make that happen; the point is to keep it front and center somewhere with all images visible. The worst idea is to have a stack of images that are left in a pile, because that will not do the job of the vision board.

Every time an idea about an area of your landscape pops into you head, jot it down on a piece of paper along with details you want to note and tack it up on the board. When flipping through a garden magazine, tear out pictures that resonate and tack them up. Take photos of yards or parks you see, or photos of pages in books, or grab screenshots from the internet, and tack those up. Allow yourself to dream out loud. As you fill the board, you will begin to see the textures, colors, patterns, and shapes to which you are drawn, which are all very important cues to what you desire. All of these are critical to creating your *wow* factor.

ONLINE VISION BOARDS

You could also create your vision board on an online vision board tool like Pinterest if that works better for you. For me, there is something about keeping my board in a physical space that allows for passive glances and edits that access the creative visioning process in a way that is deeper than when I log onto Pinterest. On the other hand, there is something to be said for being able to check your board on your phone from any location.

The next exercise will be to look at your vision board and reference your design journal and all your data to get a feel for your project direction. You are still just collecting data, but it's now in the form of a review to see how far you have come. As your vision board evolves or when you feel you have completed it, write a list of needs, wants, and wishes based on what you see on the board and what you recorded in your design journal. The following is an explanation of each to help you create your list.

> **Needs**. Hot button items—the ones that nag at you the most, bother you the most, or hold your attention so fiercely that handling these areas becomes a priority. It is important that all decision makers in your home buy into each item. If you are allocating time and attention

as well as financial resources to an area, it is best to have support in the effort. It may be the patio, fire pit, or kitchen garden that you see as a game changer for how you will enjoy your yard with your whole family.

Wants. Warm areas of interest—elements that you desire but do not feel under pressure to pursue immediately. You have patience that allows you the time to plan, save, and schedule farther out in the developmental schedule. Decision makers should agree on the concept, but the details do not need to be developed. It is okay at this stage if there is still some disagreement. An example of an element in this category might be a new front stoop and walkway. You desire it. It would be nice to have but it is just not as important as that patio you want in the backyard.

Wishes. Cool areas of interest—elements you feel may be fun or just appeal to you, but you are unsure if you are leaning into a fad or just dreaming too deeply. You may feel as though the wish is a financial pipedream or the decision makers are at total odds with one another on this one. I often see elements such as pools and spas fall into this area, as well as sport courts and putting greens. Believe it or not, even simple elements like fences and lawn areas can land in the "Wishes" category because of disagreements that arise between the decision makers.

Do your best not to overthink the needs, wants, and wishes. Just write them down because everything at this stage is flexible. You are working toward understanding your priorities and how they align with the priorities of your financial partners.

Finally, organize your images so they correspond to your needs, wants, and wishes. Throughout the process, study your images. You will learn a lot about what you like. You also want to critique your vision. Ask yourself questions about your vision board images and digital pins. For each image, ask yourself what is it that you really like about it in detail. Try to pluck them out and consider what might not work. And be okay with deciding you do not like it anymore. Be willing to move the images around, add images, and remove images. This is the process of refinement. You may look at this board for months, sometimes up to six months or more, before you take a single step toward making your vision happen.

This part of the process is important, especially if you are embarking on the design project solo! You are implanting these images in your mind to let the design evolve. Visioning never really ends so at some point it will be time to pull the trigger on designing the solution in detail. Often you can feel when the time is right. You will get itchy to have this space become a reality. Dreaming won't be enough anymore.

Top 7 Questions to Ask About Each Vision Board Image

1. What colors are prominent?

2. What textures are prominent?

3. What is the main function of this space or feature or plant?

4. What is the style of this space or feature?

5. What is my favorite feature in this image?

6. What might be a hurdle to my attaining something like this?

7. Does this image jibe with the other images or is there a conflict?

When you are ready to move forward with your vision and your wild, crazy dream, you will collect raw data about your land, such as soil conditions, hours of sun and shade, and water resources. Your dream and hard data will drive your plan and help you to map the full experience of being in your outside environment.

***

At this point I hope you truly understand the importance of giving yourself the freedom to dream up a landscape that may or may not be built as you originally pictured it. Allowing the process to unfold and evolve is the best approach. Giving yourself a deadline and some creative guideposts (like the needs, wants, and wishes) to keep you on track will set you up for the next step of collecting the practical data that will harness your vision into reality.

 TODAY'S TASKS

1. Identify your project location in your landscape (bring a notebook). Maybe drag a beach chair over there - sit and contemplate - try free association - jot what comes to mind.

2. Define the space type - Arrival/Social/Transition/ Forgotten - now list the uses and/or activities.

3. Look around - how are you getting in and out of this newly developed place in your landscape? Think of walking around the landscape and think about going in and out of the house.

4. Start collecting visual images of landscapes that resonate with all you've learned through steps 1 to 3. This will be the start of your vision board.

5

SEE YOUR SETTING

"If, then, I were asked for the most important advice I could give, that which I considered to be the most useful to the men of our century, I should simply say: in the name of God, stop a moment, cease your work, look around you."

—Leo Tolstoy, *Essays, Letters and Miscellanies*

Remember how early in my career I was an entry-level landscape helper? I mulched, weeded, and hauled wheelbarrows to and fro, which was great exercise, but that was about it. Then one day, my boss asked me to plant a row of roses in front of a stone wall along a roadside. That sounded exciting, and the roses were so pretty! He set out the 24 rose bushes along two front walls. My coworker dug the 24 holes evenly spaced at two feet apart. My job was to pop each rose out of its pot, place it in the hole, toss a handful of fertilizer around the rose, then backfill and tamp down the planting. The row of roses looked beautiful when we were done, and I felt proud of the day's work.

This property was in my hometown, so I passed my roses regularly as I drove here and there. Sadly, they never really looked as good as they had in the year that we planted them.

In time, they stopped flowering. They lost leaves and seemed to get thinner. I will never forget noticing those roses about a year or so later. They were just sad twiggy plants in front of that wall, not the vibrant plants that I remembered planting.

At the time, I didn't understand what had gone wrong, but as I look back now, I totally get it. That beautiful stone wall was an east-facing wall. For the most part it was a cool and mostly shaded location. Even though the area received beautiful morning light, over time the roses just failed to thrive in that particular environment. To make matters worse, the roadside wall collected a good amount of snow, which took a long time to melt in the spring because of that cool eastern exposure.

If you know anything about roses, you know they like sun, warmth, protection, and rich organic soil. Apparently, no one on that landscaping crew knew that back then, including me. We planted them in gravel out along that roadside. The homeowner and landscaper saw the morning sun and assumed that "sun is sun, no matter where and when it is shining" and so this place would do for roses. By choosing to plant those roses in that location we were signing their death sentence.

This kind of thing happens all the time. Landscapers are not the only perpetrators. Landscape designers and landscape architects also make this mistake. They are so eager to force a solution on an environment they miss the important cues that their choices are less than healthy for the plantings. You can imagine how easy it is for a homeowner on a weekend-warrior gardening project to make this same kind of mistake. But the good news is, it is just as easy to avoid this mistake if you take the time to learn about your environment. And that means you need to collect information.

Collecting data about the environmental elements and

existing conditions of your property is critical. The data you collect provides the building blocks for drafting an actual design plan. People working without a designer often skip this step because they often see their project as too small to require this level of work. Or worse, they do not think the job requires planning at all, and this leads to big mistakes.

I was once hired to do a site assessment for a homeowner who was interested in expanding his open lawn areas. When I got there, the client showed me the side yard where he had about 21 large oaks and pines cut down to ground level. His question was, "Where should I locate planting beds to dress up the edges?" I was a little dumbfounded that he had no next step planned for the stumps. When I shared with him that the right action was to start with pulling all the stumps, it was his turn to look at me dumbfounded. It did not occur to him that there was a next step for the tree removal. He expected to simply cut down the trees, add soil around and over the flush-cut stumps, and seed the yard. He thought I was there to help him with the design of the planting beds, rather than to identify the additional work needed. When I advised him to complete the proper preparation for the lawn area, it came as a total surprise to him and represented an investment he was not at all prepared to make.

Never skip this step of your project. It is by far the most critical piece of your planning, even if you are planting just a few flowers. Soil, sun, and water are the three most important elements. They will create constraints on your design, as well as serve as your guide for plant selection. Without understanding your unique site, you are in danger of making bad choices. These run the gamut of bad plant choices, bad placement choices, bad construction choices, and bad timing or project phasing choices. On the other hand, gathering and analyzing your data helps you make decisions that will lead to a win.

Determine Your Environmental Conditions

I cannot stress enough that you have to know your site, including the type of soil you have, how much sun you get and when, where you get your water, the existing topography of hills & valleys, and the existing vegetation. You will translate that information to support underlying structure of your living design when you create your project plan. Your data will help you work through the plant selection process and you will be on your way to success in your landscape. You can update it as conditions change on your land, such as trees that mature or light patterns that change. Once your site analysis is complete, you will want to go back to your vision to vet the viability of your ideas. Again, you do not need to concern yourself with the details when you return to your vision, but you will be surprised at how understanding the basics of your site will begin to morph your vision into your final plan.

SOIL

Soil type isn't to be taken lightly. Soil is where your plants are going to live, so just as it is critical to match sun- and shade-loving plants to the corresponding light in your yard, you need to make a good match here too. For example, plants that prefer sandy soil will fail to thrive or will outright die in a heavy, claylike soil. The same is true of plants that prefer acidic to alkaline soil. For more on plant selection and a handy site analysis worksheet, you can download my free eBook called

Picking Plants from *www.TheGardenContinuum.com.*

The first step to soil management is to assess your soil. You should take the time to assess your soil in these two ways.

- **Visual and manual assessment** is testing the physical characteristics of the soil. Dig a hole at least 6–12 inches deep, then determine the type of soil based on its structural asset. Look for the way particles of sand, silt, and clay are assembled. Sand is the largest soil particle and sandy soils feel gritty. Silt is a medium-sized soil particle and silty soils feel slippery in the hand. Clay is the smallest soil particle, so heavy clay soils feel sticky. All soil is a mixture of all three types of particles, but the dominant particle will determine the soil's properties and how plants grow within it. Then check the infiltration of root and of rock, smell the soil, and ball it up in your hand to see how it holds together. You need to be experienced to use this method alone but even a novice can tell if the soil smells bad, is full of rocks, or is generally unpleasant to dig in. The truth is that garden soil should be "easy" on some level to work with. The term "friable," meaning crumbly or easily broken into pieces, is one applied to soil in farming and pertains to landscape development and care too.

- **Soil tests** check the characteristics of the soil. The standard testing labs test the chemical and structural makeup of your soil. It is critical to understand the nutrient level, pH, organic matter, and cation exchange rate. This tests the soil's ability to hold positively charged ions, which influences soil structure stability, nutrient availability, soil pH, and the soil's reaction to fertilizers and other ameliorants. You don't want to feed your soil in a vacuum. The fact is, all agricultural operations consider their soil structure and availability first. It worries me when landscape professionals and gardeners skip this step. Understanding its chemical characteristics will help you make better decisions and, I believe, also save money and have healthier plants. Start by finding your land grant university lab. You can find it by searching "land grant universities <your state>." Avoid box tests from a garden center or home improvement store, as they are not going to give you as detailed a test result. Land grant universities all over the country provide this service along with guidelines for how to conduct the test. Follow those guidelines exactly to collect and submit your test. When you fill out the paperwork remember to check the box for organic matter analysis as well as your standard test. This may cost a little more, but the data is valuable and useful to your next steps. The soil lab will send back a report telling you about your soil characteristics. Many labs also give recommendations on how to improve the soil based on what you want to do with it, such as how to improve an area in which you plan to plant blueberries or an area you want to develop as an ornamental planting border. As an aside, you can also do biological testing, but that is too big a topic for me to dive into here. You can visit www.soilfoodweb.com for oodles of great information about the living parts of soil and their testing lab. I'll dive into a few points on this in the *Community* section later in this chapter.

Information Resources are essential tools in any gardener's toolkit. In my area, I use UMass Extension as a resource all of the time. They are always expanding their library of free information. For anyone in the northeastern U.S., this is a great resource to check out. For deeper and more focused information on specific topics, you can connect with local farming associations and ecological landscape associations and with conservation and wetland protection associations. With all the results you get, you could decide to dig out and replace your soil to change its characteristics, but I don't advise it. If you have sandy soil and want rich, loamy soil, it would take truckloads and truckloads of soil to change the conditions. And even then, if the surrounding area and the area below what you've removed is sand, this fight may be fruitless in the end. It is hard to turn a beach into a farm or woodland. It is better to look around to find plants that simply prefer what your landscape has to offer. Then apply some light amending in the form of additional nutrients and organic compost to supply the new planting with a nourishing boost in the right direction.

You can also gain clues to your soil conditions by taking notes of plants that live and thrive near your project area. If you have pines and oaks, you most likely have acidic soil. If maples and birches grow on or near your site, the soil may be more alkaline. Look at the shrubs in the area and note if they are thriving with rich, green, lush foliage and prolific flowers, or if they look yellow and weak. This may be an indicator of soil health or the lack thereof. Look to see what insect and critter pressures are being felt in your yard as well as your neighbor's yard. Don't be shy. Go see what your neighbors are doing and learn about their successes and their struggles. Most people love to talk about their gardens.

SUN

To truly understand the available sun in your garden, you need to physically go out into your space repeatedly throughout the year to gauge the sun exposure. Mapping the shade in your landscape can be a very useful exercise to know how much sun you have and to select plants to round out your design. If you want to succeed in your garden endeavors, you are going to need to know where and when you have sun. It is not as simple as seeing sun in a bed at one moment and classifying that area as sunny (remember those roses?) or seeing shade and classifying it as shady. You need to consider the angle of the sun as it moves across the sky from east to south to west throughout the day, and as the position changes with the earth's rotation on its axis through the seasons.

Determining the hours of sunlight and the angle of the sun will help you understand how the sun's rays affect your garden. If you have no trees, no house, no garage, or any other structure that could cast shade, this information would be enough. But the truth is, we all have at least one dwelling on our property that will cast shade. Many of us have trees too. And your neighbors probably have trees that may affect the light in your yard. Use this information to determine the average availability of sun and match that up to what plants want. You are probably familiar with the following sun scale used by many nurseries:

- Full sun: minimum six hours of direct sun exposure

- Part sun: four to five hours of partial sun exposure

- Part shade: three to four hours of protected sun exposure

- Full shade: less than three hours of filtered sun

This scale looks simple on paper but how about in practice? By creating a simple shade map, you will gain a clearer picture of the true level of sun exposure in your garden. Watch and map the shade patterns by checking your yard at 9 a.m., noon, and 3 p.m. This will give you three points to connect to make the arc of shade movement. To truly map your shade correctly, you need to gather data at least twice in the year. These dates are once in the summer when the sun is the highest in the sky at noon and once in the spring or fall when the sun's position is mid-sky at noon. If you really want to understand your exposure, map in all four seasons at the autumn and spring equinoxes and the winter and summer solstices. And then keep a watchful eye on changes.

This shade map is going to be very useful for planning and will continue to be an accurate shade map for about three years, five years if you push it. Beyond that time, the trees that are casting shade will have grown and their shade will increase. Or maybe you put an addition onto your house that's creating more shade. On the other hand, you could cut down the tree when it gets too big; then you will have more sun. One thing you can count on with landscape projects is that the environment is most certainly changing all the time. Plan to stay on top of data collection over time. For more information you can read the blog post *Mapping Your Shade* on my website.

WATER

Before you install a single plant, please consider where you get water, how you get water to your plants, and how easy it is for you to water them.

Source

Where is your water coming from? Is it town water or from a well? This matters because town water costs money. Well water does not (other than electricity for the pump) but it can run out. Keep in mind that many cities and towns have water bans and well water restrictions to protect the water source. Time your planting to align with weather conditions that are best to establish plants and that will allow water use. For instance, in many places, summer planting is a no-no. (The exception could be Florida and other subtropical areas with lots of summer rain.) Focus on early fall and then early spring as the best acclimation seasons to get new plants started with the least amount of shock and stress to the plant and the ecological system.

Access

How easy is it to access water? When you need water, what hurdles do you have to surmount to get it? If you have to get hoses, attach them, and drag them to the area you want to water, how likely are you to water as needed? If you have an irrigation system, is it designed to deliver water adequately to each area of the landscape? Will you set it and forget it, with no thought about whether it will water enough at some point and waste water at another?

Ease

Focus on ease of use, which may not mean full automation. It means that for each season you need to think about the water source and access. How can you design the setup for ease of use? Automated underground systems are not the only answer. Soaker hoses, timers, temporary drip lines, rain barrels, and free line spigots off your automatic underground system are just a few ways to be smart about water. Find the system that makes the most sense for you and your land and aligns with conservation practices. Just having access to water does not mean using more is the right option. The goal should be to use the least amount of water necessary in landscape management.

Define Your Limitations and Opportunities

After you collect data about your site, you will have a good idea of the limitations of your property. You'll have a clear list of what you don't have access to in the form of resources. *I have limited sun and an excess of water. I have too much sun and sandy soil.* With information like that you can limit, limit, limit your design choices. This is a very important part of the process and a good thing! Then move onto opportunities. *Okay, so I have three and a half hours of sun, rocky soil, and no access for equipment, so what would live there and how might I create this space?*

To start the process, ask yourself the following primer questions about each part of your project. You have decided to put in a patio with surrounding gardens. When you are finished answering questions about these garden elements, you might realize, "Gee, I have just the right amount of sun and I don't have any wind, so it looks like my problem is privacy. Now I know what I have to solve." And now you have the opportunity to find a creative solution for creating privacy.

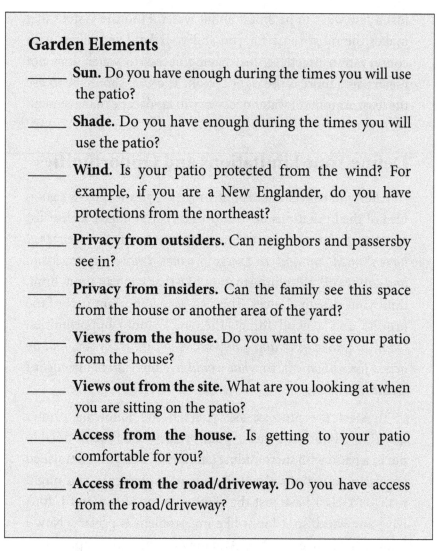

Garden Elements

_____ **Sun.** Do you have enough during the times you will use the patio?

_____ **Shade.** Do you have enough during the times you will use the patio?

_____ **Wind.** Is your patio protected from the wind? For example, if you are a New Englander, do you have protections from the northeast?

_____ **Privacy from outsiders.** Can neighbors and passersby see in?

_____ **Privacy from insiders.** Can the family see this space from the house or another area of the yard?

_____ **Views from the house.** Do you want to see your patio from the house?

_____ **Views out from the site.** What are you looking at when you are sitting on the patio?

_____ **Access from the house.** Is getting to your patio comfortable for you?

_____ **Access from the road/driveway.** Do you have access from the road/driveway?

Keep in mind that every property has the potential to be great if you work with it and let it speak to you. Every landscape can become an oasis of vibrant life, healthy foliage, colorful flowers, rich fragrances, and structural elegance. Determining this potential starts with being clear about the limitations of the site. And every property has limitations. They are not bad;

they just serve as an instructive guideline that helps you to put "banks on the river" of your creative flow so that it doesn't spread out all over the place. For example, if your property is in full sun, you are limited by that environmental condition so you cannot install shade-loving plants and expect them to thrive. Or if your soil is acidic, you do not want to put in plants that do best in an alkaline environment.

You will also find that certain site elements, such as too much or too little shade, may pose problems for the vision you created. When you encounter these obstacles, you have two choices. You can forge ahead with determination to surmount these hurdles through heavy-handed construction. Or you can shift your vision to make the outcome just as pleasing but with less need for a heavy hand in the landscaping process.

For example, you have determined your yard is a part-shade, wet environment, and your vision is for full sun-loving plants. You could forge ahead with your original vision by cutting down several trees or you can spin the situation positively. Instead, think, *I get to eliminate an enormous number of plants that will not work, which will reduce the options down to something a little bit more manageable.* Then buy a book on shade gardening and learn about all the amazing plants that *will* work. Maybe as you are flipping through the pages you realize, *Oh, in that really shady wet spot I can plant beautiful red cardinal flower* (Lobelia cardinalis) *because it loves wet feet , meaning it's happy to root in damp to intermittently wet soils, and thrives in both sun and shade garden areas.* Now you can see that what started out as a limitation becomes an opportunity.

Community

The elements I discussed in this chapter are part of a larger community. When I talk about community, I am talking about the soil food web and the larger picture of ecology. Everything is connected. Plants share not only air space; they also share soil space. Water is important, but without soil, you have a lake. Soil is important, but without water, you have a desert. We might get creeped out by bugs, but without bugs, the system does not work. Many of us love to plant trees, shrubs, and flowers that attract birds and butterflies, but without insects and caterpillars for the birds to eat, those birds will not survive. If one resource is constricted or there is an overabundance of that resource, that may tip the scales toward the death of a part of or the whole system. Maintaining sufficiency is the name of the game. You are looking for equilibrium in the system, a kind of ebb and flow of balance between the environment and plants.

When conducting a site analysis, you need to know what will be available in the resources department of soil, nutrients, sun, shade, and water. And care. You must include care because it will only be a matter of time before the wild takes over, and all of your efforts and money will be wasted. I do not want to come across as the voice of doom, but I do want emphasize that before you begin to design and build your project, you need to understand your commitment to your ecological community of which you are an intrinsic part.

***

Ideally this chapter has inspired you to go outside and "read" your existing landscape. For better or worse, the conditions that exist there now are what you are starting with and are what you have to expand upon and overcome. As you get to know what your land is really all about, you will, hopefully, be further inspired to dig into some of those characteristics to understand them better. How are gardeners dealing with shade, or with moist land, or with hot slopes? Once you pinpoint a characteristic you can zero in on limitations faster and move the process of inquiry along toward building solutions.

 # TODAY'S TASKS

1. Locate your local land grant university online. Poke around the site to find the testing lab contact and to learn about soil testing. All readers could start by checking out UMass's page for some deeper research. https://ag.umass.edu/services/soil-plant-nutrient-testing-laboratory

2. Make a list of your property's general characteristics, and then the specific characteristics of your project area. Remember, your land is diverse; the front may have different characteristics than the back.

3. Take the time to jot down the limiting factors on your site. Where are you lacking resources? This will be a critical list to refer back to later.

PART III

DIGGING IN

You are closer to picking up your shovel, but you still have a few more pieces to consider before you break ground. In Part III, I'll offer tips about how to convert all the data you collected from Part II into the bones and guts of your design. We will discuss how things get built. We will talk about the elements to consider when calculating your investment, and how to determine what amount might be reasonable for you to invest. Reading these chapters will empower you to move away from a haphazard and rushed approach to landscape projects toward a planned and measured type of landscape development.

6

PICTURE YOUR PLAN

*"Give me six hours to chop down a tree and I will spend
the first four sharpening the axe."*

—Abraham Lincoln

If it feels cool with you to be completely surprised by the end result of your gardening efforts, then by all means forge ahead without a plan. For me, working without a plan would be unacceptable. From my experience, the number one reason the do-it-yourselfer breaks down and calls a landscape professional is because the crescendo of frustration from working without a plan becomes insurmountable.

The complaint I often hear is, "It just never comes out the way I want it to!"

I then ask, "What did you want the end product to look like?" and "Did you have a plan?"

Almost 100 percent of the time, clients answer "No," followed by their explanation of what their landscape should or should not be. They don't have a defined vision. There is no plan. There is a disconnect between their dream and their real-life conditions. When this disconnect becomes obvious after the work begins, after an investment in time and materials, then corrective actions are almost always painful. That's why I'm so adamant about planning. It's my secret weapon, and now it's yours.

When you consider Yogi Berra's wise statement, *"If you don't know where you are going, you will end up someplace else,"* you will understand the importance of identifying your destination in order to get there. You may be able to imagine what could happen without a plan; you simply might not get there. That is, you will end up somewhere else entirely. It is so much more satisfying to start with a plan and be surprised when the outcome not only meets but surpasses your expectations. The outcome for those professionals and homeowners alike who dive in without a plan is often not even close to their dream. That is because the dream and the specific details of the dream need defining. And that definition starts with the envisioning process described in chapter 4. The process of visualization solidifies the feelings and emotions that go along with your dream.

Visualization is not the same as dreaming, list-making, or data collecting. Think of it this way: dreams tend to be more feeling-based desire without actually seeing a picture in your mind's eye. Lists of needs, wants, and wishes are like a shopping list that will eventually fill out that picture. Data collection is a list of the conditions you have to work with.

Visualization, on the other hand, is a tool you can use to capture those bits of information that will inform the finished aesthetic picture of what you want to develop. A vision starts to take form in your imagination using your dream (the feeling) with the lists and data (the details) you've now collected to feed the picture form of your Life-Scape. But that is not enough to start building. It is a very good idea to also think out into the future existence of this vision. Ask how it will evolve. Will the vision stand up to 20 years of time? Maybe you can try to poke holes in your plan. Ask yourself, "What could go wrong? Will having trees in that location make sense when they are huge? What could trip me up? Is there any future work needed that would upset this project I'm building now? How could this project end up taking more time or costing more money?"

The goal is to start strong and smart. Let's face it, if you are diving into the project, whether on your own or with professional assistance, you want the process to be as pain-free as possible. Better yet, how about going for pleasurable!

Stages of Landscape Maturation

Before you map your project, consider how your landscape will evolve over time. I like to break down the evolution of a landscape into four phases.

Evolution of a Landscape

- First year: New landscape
- Years 2–10: Managed landscape
- Years 11–19: Mature landscape
- Years 20-plus: Aged landscape

Landscapes are dynamic. Plants grow, environmental conditions change, and sunny areas become shady as trees mature. Your family needs change as the kids grow—a new swing set goes up, then your family grows more, and the swing set comes down. Landscape development is a process, not a project. This process has many large and small projects in it, and when you fold in the necessary ongoing care, this process is ongoing. When you create a vision and then create your plan, you are aiming for a common thread that will run through the successive phases of your landscape. Here's what these different landscape stages look like.

FIRST YEAR: NEW LANDSCAPE

The first year is unique. Your landscape is brand new. It is acclimating, getting over its planting shock, and adjusting to its new environment. During this year you are babysitting your landscape by keeping it under a watchful eye. You might water with an automatic irrigation system and augment that with some watering by hand. Weeding between the new, young plants that haven't yet filled in as planned is important. And touching up mulch to keep a protective covering on the land where plants have to grow to fill in makes good management sense. But overall, you let it be. No pruning or shearing, and no heavy fertilizing because you may have amended the soil when preparing the planting beds. There seems to be a common impulse to prune and feed in that first year, but if you installed the right plants correctly, it is not necessary. There is also an impulse to mulch heavily as a way to control weeds. Yes, you do need mulch in the beginning, but you are also going to have to weed because you want to avoid burying your new plants in mulch, which would smother the roots and soil biology.

YEARS 2–10: MANAGED LANDSCAPE

During these years you will manage your landscape and guide it to maturity. In this phase, weeding, edging, and pruning become important. In the first three years, plants are establishing feeder and stabilizing roots. They are making this new place their home. In so doing, they may grow like a teenager in a gangly fashion. Light-handed, selective pruning can shape funky growth spurts and woody structures to help the maturing process. Not all plants will establish at the same rate. Some will acclimate so fast that they start establishing when other plants are still working through the stress and shock of acclimation. This means you will see varying growth rates. With herbaceous plants in particular (perennials, annuals, and bulbs) you will see some becoming thugs while others might limp along. Manage those thugs by pruning, trimming, and dividing while you nurture the slower plants with some extra water or nutrient support. The point is, just like teenagers, they may misbehave a little. Give them time and love and be patient while they sort themselves out.

During this phase, you will need to manage invading plants such as weeds, volunteers, and invasive species with the most vigilance. A new landscape is in a disturbed state, meaning you disrupted an existing ecological system and set up a new one. It takes time for that system to recalibrate and become self-sustaining. Until your landscape becomes self-sustaining and your plants fill in, invaders will try to grab hold and take up residence. Vigilance during this period is key to long-term success and to set up ease of care during the third phase of the mature landscape. Be sure that you don't slack on the weeding!

YEARS 11–19: MATURE LANDSCAPE

During years 11–19, your landscape is in the maturing phase. This is the time when you will see where you may have veered off course a bit. For example, you might think, "Oh, damn. I should have managed those weeds better. Now they are all entangled in my groundcover, so I have unplanned work to do and choices to make." You can painstakingly separate these plants from the weeds, which often means digging the area out and teasing the weeds out from the plants. Another corrective action is simply chock it up to a loss and remove the plants along with the invading weeds and start over in that section. That is often my go-to answer. Or you may discover that in the hopes of fast privacy, you planted a few too many shrubs and now they are crowding one another out. When you stand back and look, you realize you could simply cull out every other plant, and allow the remaining ones to fill in. Not a bad choice in this phase, especially if you can repurpose the culled plants in a new location. And if you're not able to make that choice, don't feel bad about it. Sometimes getting rid of plants is just the right choice. You need a thick skin to garden!

You may feel that an old tree you left in place is starting to decline and will need to be removed. You plant a new tree in a location nearby where it can thrive just long enough to grab a foothold before you remove the older tree. This is the phase during which your foundation plantings may have matured well. They now require focused pruning on a yearly basis at the appropriate time to keep the overall height and width in check. It may be that now is the time to divide all your daylilies and irises and refresh the planting with some added space and new cultivars. The extra divisions can fill in some new open space or serve as great offerings to friends and family. The work in this phase tends to be less about weeding and more about plant management. Although I hate to break the news to you, weeds always work their way into the equation, too.

TWENTY-PLUS YEARS: AGED LANDSCAPE

After 20 years, your landscape is considered aged. It is in the grown-up phase and requires a gentle hand. You don't really have to do a whole lot. There will still be weeds here and there, but the work is generally less pressing. You will want to maintain the edges between lawn and landscape beds because there will always be a little battle going on for territory in this "edge" domain. Mulching may be to touch up every two years or so because plants have grown in so nicely. You might even hand-water if your area is experiencing a drought. Direct water only to those plants that need it so you give them just enough to make it through the dry spell; although by this time, these plants are stable and might not even need water.

There may be some flaws in the landscape, but at this point the flaws are the flaws. If you didn't put in the work during years two to ten, and if you didn't do any corrective action in years 11–19, at 20-plus years it is what it is. On the other hand, you could take corrective action with your aged landscape; just know that it will be expensive. You could apply a common restaurant or hotel rating system of putting dollar signs at each stage to indicate how expensive it can get.

Cost of Correcting

- First year: $
- Years 2–10: $$
- Years 11–19: $$$
- Twenty-plus years: $$$$

Planning for All Phases

Your goal is to minimize additional or unnecessary costs as your landscape evolves. Pay attention. If you see something that needs correcting in the early years of your landscape's life, it is best to correct it then. If you don't pay attention in the 2–10-year phase, you will pay for it in the 11–19-year phase, either by being unhappy with your landscape or paying a lot more to fix it.

I've always considered our home to be our "forever house," meaning that my husband and I plan on living in our home for the rest of our lives. It is our family home. When we began remodeling our house and developing the landscape, we made all our plans with that thought in mind. We also wanted to consider the maturation of the plants. We thought about how our family needs would evolve when we had kids, as they grew older, and later, maybe wanting places for our grandkids to play.

Different ways of thinking about your home will require different planning strategies. When you begin your project you might think, "I'll just be here for five years, because that is how long I want to be in my current job." Or, "I want to be here for five years, then I want to upgrade to more land, more house, and a pool." In both of these short-term examples, you'll want to plan with resale in the forefront of your mind. Alternatively, you may think, "I'll be in this house for 20 years until my kids are done with their schooling, and then I am leaving for Florida." Or, "I'll live in this house until they haul me out in a pine box, which is hopefully far in the future." If that is the case, then you will know that you need to build for the long-term. You can make a decision to plant a tree to give you future shade on your patio knowing it won't serve you well right now or even in five years, but as you round 10 years it will be perfect. Of course, you also have to think out about what it will look like in 20 and maybe 30 years to get the right placement. Too close and it could lift the patio with its roots. Planning for the short-term, mid-term, and long-term are all required when you are developing land for use over the long haul.

That long-term investment requires long views. And long views require that we respect the nature of the plant. If you are planting an oak tree, and you know that the base of that oak tree can grow to be 3 feet in diameter, it is a little bit different than planting a pear tree or a honey locust, because they won't grow to be nearly as large. Your choices then relate to the term of that investment. If the term is ten years, you can make one set of decisions. For example, if you are looking for shade, you might invest in awnings, umbrellas, or even a pergola with a shade cover instead of planting trees, because ten years is barely long enough to truly reap the benefits of a tree canopy. If the term is fifty years, you might want to make a different set of decisions. For example, you might strategically plant trees where you can eventually count on their canopies to shade the hottest times of the day while allowing sun in at the cooler times of day. While you wait, you may employ the assistance of a nice cantilevered umbrella that you can move to track the sun and offer shade until the trees fill in.

SUCCESSION

When planning for the evolution of your landscape, you want to weave a common thread through each phase. Let's consider the need for privacy. You may know you are going to be in your home for many years, and what you would really like is to create a beautiful green wall of plants that perfectly screen your home from your neighbors. Your lot is wide open, and to plant that many plants would be very expensive. Even though a fence would be cheaper, the idea of being penned in by a fence is entirely displeasing to you.

One solution would be to build your privacy over time. Here's how the common thread would work: You want privacy, always. That is the common thread that runs through your project over time.

1. For the first year or so, you establish the bones. You delineate the property line to suggest the privacy by putting in your infrastructure—a simple planting of tall shade trees. You will also add an infrastructure of understory evergreens to buy you ten to fifteen years of coverage. At which point, when the shade trees have grown and expanded, you may decide to remove them.

2. In a couple more years, as the trees grow in, you can see where holes remain in your screen. To deal with this you can add structural plantings—focal point flowering trees and ornamental shrubs to bring in more color and

texture. These plants should be planned and placed in such a way that they are compatible long-term with the canopies of the shade trees. Be mindful to create depth within the bed. Don't line up your plants with military precision—stagger them. Of course, this type of screen is not a solution for a small lot or a lot where the house is close to the lot line. You need plenty of room so a minimum bed width of 12 to 15 feet will be best.

3. Next, you will see gaps in color and texture, so fill in those gaps with enhancements like layers of smaller shrubs, perennials, groundcovers, and spring-flowering bulbs to offer more color and seasonal interest. Some of these plants could be transitional, filling a need for five to ten years, and then moved or removed as the environment changes.

4. In subsequent years, you may add more enhancements, and start planting more perennials, groundcovers, or bulbs that will naturalize and expand your season to give you even more excitement and diversity.

Keep in mind when you first plant those few big shade trees, they won't create a lot of privacy, but after twenty years and several strategic plantings later, you will have perfect privacy that is diverse, beautiful, and perfectly layered. In the beginning, the gaps might bother you a bit. Remember, in the garden development process you will often get what you want in stages over time rather than all at once. The bottom line is the finished product that will provide your perfect privacy. The super cool thing about this kind of layering is that it not only gets you the desired screening, it also becomes its own ecosystem and habitat for wildlife.

In a solution such as this, it is important to look at those first shade trees as permanent infrastructure elements. Ideally, you will plant them as a forever part of the overall privacy solution. As I mentioned, evergreens may be seen more as filling a good number of years in the screen but not as permanent features. Once they are tall and full, they will be just the right size for your screen. But somewhere around the 20-year mark, the mature phase of the lifecycle of this privacy screen, some of the evergreens may start thinning out or failing from the reduction in sun availability. You might just have to go in, thank them, and then cull the evergreens that aren't doing well, which may create a few gaps in your privacy.

Another approach is simply to start out by thinking of specific plants in your plan as having a finite life in the landscape. For example, blue spruces are beautiful trees that are awesome when they are young. But when they get to about 30 feet tall, at about fifteen years or so, they become too big for (most) residential landscapes. You may be thinking, wait a minute here, earlier in this book you said no hacking away at the plants to make them fit. That's still true. What makes this approach different is that you are selectively identifying some plants that may not be useful in the landscape for the long term. This allows you to confidently remove them rather than improperly prune them. Space in the residential landscape can get tight and while blue spruces are lovely plants when they're young, they get leggy as they age. They start to lose the fullness of their branching on the bottom and lose the needles on the inside. From a human scale, or what we call a pedestrian scale at eye level when you are walking, they are no longer enjoyable because all the beauty is way up at the tips of the branches where it is a stunning light blue. At that point, I would recommend cutting it down, pulling or grinding the stump out, and planting a new one if you still have enough available sunlight.

I encourage you not to look at this as a waste. It is a wise expense and a valuable move because you are replacing a tree that is no longer beautiful with a tree you will love having in your yard, at a minimal investment. While conservationists may hate me for this suggestion, I would argue that this decision reinvigorates that lower-story habitat niche for birds and other critters that may be missing that functional branching for nesting and bug hunting.

Cutting down a spruce tree, grinding down or pulling out the stump, and planting a new tree might be a $1,500 investment. That $1,500 is going to get you ten more years with a new tree, which works out to $150 a year. That is the same as a pair of solid work boots, or a killer dress, or a rototiller, all of which you might drop $150 or more on without batting an eyelash. Just give yourself permission to spend that money on a new tree and a functional solution to invigorate the landscape. Of course, you need to weigh the pluses and minuses for you and your family. You are the one who knows what will work best for you. All that said, cutting down trees may be too bold for you or too involved. If that is the case, select plants that age well. And plants that will age in a way you can live with happily ever after.

CHANGING FAMILY NEEDS

Just as I divide the phases of a landscape into ten-year chunks, I like to think of evolving lifestyle needs the same way. With kids, for example, you get a playset when the kids are little. After they get to a certain age, that playset just isn't that interesting anymore. So the playset goes and you put in a basketball court. That basketball court may last forever because the kids are totally into it, or it may age out because they just don't play basketball anymore. Next, you rip out the basketball court and you put in a really cool campfire setting with a rustic stone patio and loose boulder pit where you can build a fire. Or maybe that area with the playset is a nice sunny spot so you build a few raised beds and finally get that veggie and herb garden going that you always wanted but never had time for when you were chasing kids.

The design elements within your landscape may change from playset, to basketball court, to campfire, to veggie patch but the goal for that destination in your landscape doesn't change. The design still fills the need of the program, which suggests, "I want to get people together in this space to enjoy the activity." A common interest I see after your kids are grown is how to get your family back to the nest once they have left. What draws them back?

Maybe you don't have kids, but you want to age in your home forever. You don't want to pull up stakes and move to Florida or Costa Rica when you retire. You don't even want to move to a condo across town. If you stay in your house, at some point you will most likely want to downsize your gardens. Maybe you will replace your vegetable garden or cutting garden with native shrubs or blueberries, a straightforward project that a production level garden professional could take care of inexpensively. Again, the design will evolve along with you.

Getting It Down on Paper

If you are doing the project yourself, your plan will most likely be some sort of schematic drawing of what you are going to build. If you are working with a professional designer and contractor, your final plans will be far more refined and complete. The professional designer will work with you, coaching you through the entire process. It will be painless for you, but you do need to make yourself available to dream and work the vision with them. Remember how important you are to the process. The worst thing you can do is to disengage. This is your home so it needs your heart in the process if you have any hope of connecting with it. The second mistake is to think the designer is going to get it perfect on the first try. Remember, this is a relationship between you, the designer, and the land. It will take a bit of time to evolve and grow. The fun begins as your design plan starts to take shape because you start to see your dream take form.

During the mapping process, there are a few key elements you need to weave in to turn your vision into a concrete goal. These elements will be the functionality you are expecting such as a play space for kids or a patio that integrates well with the kitchen because you like to eat dinner outside. To determine functionality, you will also need to define access and circulation. If you are working with a designer, that job falls to them but it is in partnership with you.

Normally, the drawings are of the finished project vision. They represent that original dream made real through vetting all the concepts and ideas against the reality of your site and then plotting that final goal on paper. These plan documents do not include information about the construction details needed to build the plan. So how do we make sure that your vision is sound, can be built, and will last? We break it all down.

MAPPING YOUR PROJECT

Not all projects need to be formally designed, but they all need to be designed in some manner. In this stage, you take the vision you develop and map out all of its elements on paper or on the land. By that, I mean you need to map out every project either in a narrative list of steps, a bubble diagram, or the more tactile "design on the land" method of marking the actual landscape dimensions and features right out on the land with stakes, string, and spray paint. Or you can use a combination of these three, doing anything that will help you move from "idea" to the three-dimensional space. This exercise will uncover flaws in the plan and missed opportunities that might be great to include in the project. Every feature needs to be deciphered. That means getting clear about the sizes and quantities for each element, its placement, and the order of those elements on the land while considering the order of their construction.

Ideally, you will create an initial sketch as a simple way to get your vision on paper. It doesn't have to be perfect or accurate at first. The idea of designing scares some people, but don't let it frighten you. Designs can start off as simple as hand-drawn sketches that will eventually become a drawing on graph paper whose scale is dimensional. The vision may need to manifest on paper first before it manifests as part of your home. This is how you will begin to see the layout more clearly.

Next, as you refine your sketch you will start to fill in some of the details. These details can be as simple as the length and width of the patio, distance from the house, and features that you plan to build into or place on the patio. You will plot the garden layouts including the shapes of the bed lines, locations of trees, and special elements such as a small water feature. If you can plot these layouts to scale on paper, great!

If you feel that your paper layout is too abstract, go outside with some stakes, string, flags, and landscape-safe white marking paint, and mark out the patio, the bed line shapes, and the location of trees. This way you can get your vision into a 3D-view to really picture it. You can even stand in it and start to feel how the space is shaping up. Then drawing it to scale using real dimensions will help the designs make more sense to you.

Going through this exercise of spraying out a deck or patio and staking out trees with clients is great fun for me. I love their reactions when they see their patio take form—the shape, size, location, access to the house, and even where the grill might be simply painted on the ground. A little time and some paint are about as easy and inexpensive as it gets. Yes, it takes time to do this, but the payoff is awesome! Some clients want to drag their existing furniture into the spray-out patio to really "feel" it. Oftentimes, we end up adding a foot or two of width or length to the patio or deck because that little extra space goes a long way in comfort. When you can "step" into the design, you can decide, "Yeah, I want a little more space here." You can use this process with any elements of your landscape such as staking out trees, determining how wide to make your beds, drawing a pathway, or even laying out a driveway and driving on it like I did!

An amazing thing happens when you start to map out your plan. Your vision becomes more real as you begin the process of vetting its viability for construction. In the visioning phase you may have dreamed up a big patio with lots of living spaces, maybe a hot tub and a campfire area. But when you go outside to the project location, you notice a slope that presents a problem for your large patio idea. You realize you have to consider how to flatten the land, a small retaining wall perhaps. Or you may shift your vision to incorporate two smaller patio terraces on the slope. Your vision will evolve as you take the time to get out there to really see it.

Getting Real—Being a Realist May Be Your Best Bet for Success

The design process is a slippery slope if it's not kept in check. First, it is very easy to overdesign by cramming too many functions in one space. It is one of the dangers of looking for inspiration in garden centers and big-box stores. It is also easy to add features because they are trending or popular. That is part of the danger of doing research on popular design resource websites. I call this "Feature-Scaping." Finally, if you aren't careful, you will spend all your time designing and never get to building. That is the danger of aiming for picture-perfect. I have learned to sidestep these traps over decades of developing my personal property and teaching, consulting, designing, building, and maintaining landscapes. Let's dive into a few of the pitfalls that I want to help you to avoid along your project-planning journey to ensure that you're successful.

OVERDESIGN

Overdesign is a common mistake that happens when you don't consider the house itself when designing a landscape. For instance, you decide to incorporate an outdoor dining area because it can be romantic and relaxing to have a meal under the stars. I suggest that step one would be to think about where this table will be in proximity to the other tables in your house for eating. Modern kitchens often include a breakfast nook, a bar with stools, or a freestanding table. In many homes, I see kitchen tables that have a view of dining room tables that look out onto deck tables. Nobody *sits* that much nowadays, never mind *dining* that much! The point is to avoid creating redundancies in the design that make for a boring view. The ideal would be to develop views outward that are a little different from the viewing platform. In other words, sitting at a table, looking at a table—yawn. Sitting at a table, looking at a set of comfy lounge chairs with a side table with a couple of big planters overflowing with flowers in the sunshine—take me there, please!

Set up the functional areas in your landscape so they complement the inside experience as well as one another on the outside rather than repeat or confuse one another. Just as with rooms in your house that have specific and possibly related functions—kitchen, dining, sitting, lounging—you can achieve that same effect on the outside. And while I get that cooking and eating inside versus doing those activities outside are somewhat different, I'd like you to try to stagger the views so that you can really enjoy looking out your windows. All it takes is a little patience and creativity to skew a patio left or right or to bump out a deck four feet off the kitchen windows as a way to push views in your favor.

FEATURE OVERLOAD

The landscape industry is so popular now that magazines, home and garden shows, and big-box store promotions are constantly telling us what we need. Take a fire pit, for example. One day it is a must-have item, the next, it is out of fashion. I've had several new clients tell me that their built-in fire pit or fireplace has never really been incorporated into their lifestyle.

They want to know how to make the place more usable, often asking about moving or removing the feature. The truth is that fewer than half the fire pits I see in landscapes are used regularly. Why is that?

My hypothesis is that while fire pits and fireplaces are incredibly romantic and alluring features to sit beside with friends and family while drinking hot cocoa with marshmallows, they are also work. Someone has to stock wood for that fire, build that fire, tend that fire, and then clean up after that fire. This work is not a bad thing at all, if you are the fire-building, -tending, -stocking type or if you live with one. If no one wants to shoulder the work or orchestrate a team effort, then it just doesn't get done.

Features like this are everywhere in the landscape: pools and spas, putting greens and sport courts, ponds and water features, and, oh, don't get me started on outdoor kitchens. These elements are fun if you use them, but more often they just add to your workload. And let's face it, we've become a very busy society. If you have a pool, kitchen, spa, fire pit, and patio, the chores add up. Even outdoor furniture requires work. Cushions need to be brought in, washed, and stored for the off-season. This is just the reality of having them. The weather beats them up and takes its toll, especially in my neck of the woods. There is no rest for the weary here in New England! The key is to know the amount of maintenance involved before you dive into installing any one of these features, and to be sure that the feature is "you." If you are a fireside-kinda boy or a Jacuzzi-kinda girl, taking care of one of these features will be a part of your daily, weekly, and monthly activities. And if you want to hire service providers to do the work for you, just know we are here for you, but those costs add up.

PERFECTION PARALYSIS

Dreams are blurry and fluid. Allow them to be imperfect and dreamy. If things float in and out of the dream, that is okay. The point is to start locking things down in your vision, which is a little more refined than your dream. And your plan is more refined than the vision. And your final design should be locked down. You need to know when to *stop* adding. If you are still adding, then you might not have completed your visioning.

Anyone who has embarked on the design journey, knows how "refinement" can cause you to stall in the process. You have an idea. You start to implement it. You rethink it. You develop a new idea, which involves a new approach altogether, and before you know it, you are playing musical chairs with plants and rocks, and it is anyone's guess where they will land. This is as true for designing a landscape as it is for designing a kitchen, or a website for your business, or even designing a book! I've done them all. The key is to put a stake in the ground, stop designing, and get to building.

A surefire way to get caught in this bind is to choose elements such as plants, furniture, and features before you solve the fundamental foundation of design. The vision you create will be tethered to the data you uncover about your project site, which we cover in the next chapter, and that connection will help to limit your design choices. That is a good thing! Why? Because you will strive to be more creative in your solutions. "Less is more" works in the landscape. It focuses your effort and your investment into the highest value elements that will get you the biggest return on use and in resale value.

We talked about limitations in chapter 5. I just want to reiterate that limitations and boundaries are good to have. They narrow your choices and force you to focus on one thing. When designing, you want to get simple, not complex. Solve one layer at a time. Think about function, because function rules. What will you do in this place you design? What is its function? Ideally, it is one activity or a few related activities. Don't cook where you swim, swim where you eat, or eat where you play basketball. Focus. Each room in your house has an assigned central purpose or related purposes, so design your landscape in the same way. You can get creative later and convert the space for multiple uses. But when you are designing, you want to drill down to one function per space as a way to get clarity.

LAST THINGS FIRST

The other important rule of design is to understand the underlying infrastructure first. These are the hard elements of the property that are difficult or impossible to change. Then identify the structural bones of your landscape. These are the elements that may already be in place but can be changed. From there you will work your way up to choosing the decorative enhancements that will make people go "ooh" and "aah." These are the easy elements that tend to be the ones that got us thinking about this project in the first place!

Think about your house as an example. Few people think about the infrastructure of the house that allows them to design and furnish rooms. The skeletal framework of the house is what everything else rests on or is built from. The electrical wiring allows you to have lights and kitchens appliances. Your landscape also needs the base infrastructure.

Start with non-plant infrastructure such as the utilities, the landform, and the hardscape elements for access, and the infrastructural plants such as the massive trees that will change the fabric of your landscape over time. Next, work on the structures in the landscape like the hardscape and large plants that affect selected areas of your landscape by changing views, creating spaces for gathering, for closure, sightline management, and for circulation. Last, you'll finalize the plan with fun plant and décor enhancements that bring that sparkle to the landscape so that it feels like an artful expression—the wow.

Infrastructure

- **Deciduous trees:** maple, oak, beech, elm, ash, sweetgum, hickory, pecan, and so forth

- **Evergreen trees:** hemlock, pine, spruce, fir, redwood, arborvitae, and so forth

- **Non-Plant:** All utilities (in-ground and above), septic systems, wells, irrigation, driveways, main step ways and retaining walls, safety lighting, roads, and all manner of build dwelling structures

Plant and Hardscape Structure

- **Trees:** cherry, crabapple, magnolia, dogwood, maple, redbud, and so forth

- **Shrubs:** rhododendron, laurel, viburnum, lilac, yew, winterberry, witch hazel, and so forth

- **Non-Plant:** walks, patios, pools, sitting and decorative walls, fences, décor lighting

Plant and Décor Enhancements

- **Plants:** perennials, groundcovers, bulbs, vines, and annuals

- **Non-Plant:** all art pieces, water features, planters, arbors, and select décor

When a design is driven by the enhancements, that design will be weak and flimsy. To avoid this weakness, drive with the infrastructure as your road map, the structure as your vehicle, and the enhancements weighing in as the elements of fun and excitement.

The best rule of thumb I can offer here is, "infrastructure first, enhancements last." By layering in these pieces throughout your entire landscape, putting in one layer immediately after the other, you ensure a strong design. If budget or time is an issue, the landscape project can be developed in layers over a few seasons. I've installed many landscapes where we get through the infrastructure and part of the structure in one year, then complete the structural work and the enhancements in the next year. And of course, many landscapes need to be built over several years, like mine! In that case, you'd treat each section you are building as a complete project—starting with the infrastructure elements and working through structure and finishing with the enhancements before moving onto the next. You also want to make sure to start in the back or the hardest space to access on your land. After you complete that area, you can move up toward the next location continuing this process until you have completed your project.

Note that whenever you phase a project you increase its cost because you lose some of the savings you would get from the all-at-once construction. But that is okay. My husband and I have been building our home and landscape over the past twenty years, and we are getting *everything* we want, just one or a few elements at a time.

***

You can see how important creating your plan is to your project. It is my hope that by helping you see the fun in creating your vision from your dream and then developing your plan, you will see how satisfying the whole planning process can be *and* how it can work to build excitement rather than extinguish it.

 # TODAY'S TASKS

1. Start to imagine your final project outcome. You need to close your eyes to do this well. Focus on the space, the features, the use, and see yourself in the space.

2. Identify the state of maturity of your present landscape as a way to tether your vision back to reality. Do they line up easily?

3. Note your personal/family stage and how long you think you'll be in this house as a way to determine best solutions and guide your investments.

4. Create a first map of your project, a loose sketch to capture the biggest elements. Keep it simple and focus on the use and function of each feature.

BUILD IT

"Individual commitment to a group effort—that is what makes a team work, a company work, a society work, a civilization work."

—Vince Lombardi

Once you have a schematic that shows the parts of your project, locations of the parts, and details of the parts, you can see your vision more clearly as a finished product in your existing landscape.

The result of your planning should be that when you stand at your door you actually see the shadow of this new landscape taking shape. Then comes the big question: How will all these ideas become reality? When you reach the building phase of your project, you might start feeling a bit frightened. You may think, "Ugh. This is too big, or too expensive, or it will take forever." Or you may feel a sense of nervous excitement.

It's time for you to take a breath and break down your project further. You are almost there but you are not starting the actual building yet. Instead, you are going through all of the steps of building on paper, which includes imagining your team and the project workflow. For this final phase before production, you need to define three distinct segments:

- Who's going to build it?

- How much time you will spend?

- How much money you will need?

These segments aren't necessarily linear but starting with "who's going to build it" makes the most sense. If you are doing the work, you will be the one to outline the timeline and budget. If you are managing the project, you will most likely interview several professionals to select the one or the ones you like best. During that interview process, make sure to cover the timeline and budget. After you determine who will build it, you will move back and forth through the second and third segments: nailing down (1) the time you will personally invest including putting a value on your time, and (2) the amount you will need to invest in outside labor and materials. Your time and money are the two major investments in building a project. Consider both as equally important resources for developing your dream.

Decide Who Is Building Your Project

Deciding who will build your project is an important step in mapping the timeline of your projects and determining your financial investment. To determine who will build the project, you need to know three things:

- Your personal avatar—Actor, Director, or Audience (see chapter 3)

- The type of project you are undertaking—Do It Yourself, Divide and Conquer, Hands off and Watch. See "Project Types" (following)

- The level of tradesperson you will be partnering with— Producer, Method, or Mastery (see chapter 3)

From my professional and personal experience, I can tell you with 100 percent certainty that garden-making, big or small, is a collaborative effort. There is no doing the work all by yourself. Even if you are out there on your own, digging soil, setting stones, planting plants, you *are* in collaboration with nature. The truth is, most projects that result in wonderful, enjoyable outside spaces are complex works of creativity, construction, and care. More than one person is most often involved. Remember, collaboration, transparency, and patience are necessary for a positive experience and outcome. I've been doing this for a lifetime, and I know that nothing beats a great team pulling in the same direction. Okay, now on to the process.

YOUR AVATAR

After reading about garden avatars in chapter 3, you know what type of role you will fill in your project. I suggest rereading that description to make sure it is still resonating with you.

PROJECT TYPES

There are three main ways that any project can be built:

- **Do-It-Yourself (DIY).** These projects may cost less financially, but always cost more in time. Remember, you are investing sweat equity in lieu of dollars.

Additionally, these projects have a physical cost. Be honest with yourself when it comes to assessing your ability both physically and in terms of skill level with equipment. Don't forget to consider mental fortitude. Nothing frustrates the human psyche more than the work of manipulating nature to succumb to our whim and will!

- **Divide and Conquer (DAC).** You may spend more than you would on a DIY project, and the project will likely go a bit faster because you have help. They also require less physical and skill-building investment. This approach allows you to partner with professionals who can fill a skill and muscle gap beyond what you bring to the project. Together, you will invest your time and sweat equity to build the parts of the project that you feel the best suited for while leaning on professional contractors to do the heavy lifting of building infrastructure and structure. Additionally, when things don't go exactly as planned or when new opportunities pop up, you now have partners in thinking and troubleshooting which can be a true blessing.

- **Handoff and Watch (HAW).** Assuming you are comparing the same project across these build options, these projects cost the most and are generally the fastest to complete. This approach may also be the most relaxing, because you have completely handed off your project to a trusted contracting company that will have your best interests in mind when building. For the most part, you will not be bothered with the project troubleshooting. This partner will be highly capable and interested in keeping you well informed and confident of their ability to deliver the result you desire.

PARTNERS

Remember, this book is not teaching you how to build any landscape feature. To build your project, you will need to either learn the skills on your own or partner with someone who has them. Even if you do learn the skills, I am going to reiterate that there is huge value in collaboration, both in refining the design and in the methods used to build the project. I've been blessed to work with amazing contractors who help me see that one additional item or element of a feature can be refined. Even as a seasoned designer, I love the collaborative energy sparked from discussing the design features and project approach with fellow professionals. I think this is often a missed opportunity in the landscape development process.

I discussed the three types of professionals you might partner with in chapter 3 under the heading "Finding Garden Partners: Who's Out There to Help You." If that section isn't fresh in your mind, I suggest you review it.

Determine How Much Time You Will Invest

Your first step in determining the investment level for your project is to decide how much time will be needed over the duration of the project. To do that, you need to decide whether yours is an all-at-once project or if you are going to build it in phases.

An all-at-once project means you have access to all the necessary resources of both time and money to invest in the work. On one end of the spectrum, this may mean you are hiring contractors to get the project done quickly and you can easily afford that investment. At the other end of the spectrum, you are doing the work yourself and have all the time you need to build all of the features of the project.

Another option you might choose is to build your project in phases, one part at a time. Building in phases could look like building the deck and surrounding structural plants in year one. The next year, you might take on the new walkway, front stoop, and foundation plantings. Finally, in the following year comes that dream pond garden with a glorious waterfall. This is a common and highly viable approach under two circumstances:

- **Limited clarity.** You are only clear about one part of your overall project and need to see it finished to gain clarity on the next parts. A design for a large space consists of a number of moving parts. You may have a clearly developed vision and plan for the back yard, while the front yard hasn't made it past a first-pass concept. You don't need to wait until the design is totally complete to start building. But you do need to have a strong overall concept developed so you can be smart about which part of the project should come first. From there, you can start building one part of your project, and save parts two and three for a later day. Clarity about those parts will come as the first part unfolds and becomes a reality.

- **Limited resources.** You just don't have the time or money to invest in building the project all at once. Chris and I developed our land over time as we could afford each project. This worked really well for us. How did we determine which to build first? We focused on the "trouble" areas first. We planted trees to shield the house from the sun. We knew they would take many years to do that job, so getting them in first was key. Then we focused on that crazy runway of a driveway. It bothered us and it was so ugly, so it had to change. This was on the top on our NEEDS list. But that is just one way to phase your project. Others include starting with a living area of the landscape. For you it may be getting the deck right, which is a super place to start because, technically, while it is in the landscape, it is also very much a part of your house. It should come before patio. Or maybe for you it is the arrival experience and getting a comfortable front stoop. Then you move on to building a welcoming front walk for you and your guests that makes your home look inviting and provides curb appeal.

Because time and money are the two main investment resources needed to build any project, be certain you are clear about how much of each resource you need before you start your project. You don't want the supply of these critical elements to run dry before you are finished.

RESPECTING YOUR RESOURCES

Time, like money, is a resource that doesn't "grow on trees." Just because you want a project to take less time, doesn't mean it will. Nagging and pressuring your contractor to complete a project faster when there have been real measurable delays such as weather or material changes isn't constructive or kind. Wishing for a project to cost less doesn't work either. The message is to respect both these resources as limited and precious. Giving a project the resources it needs is paramount to success. Planning is how you set expectations before construction starts.

We all know that cutting corners to save money will often bite you in the backside in the end. What is not quite as obvious is that rushing a project can cause your project to fail, either immediately or down the road. Rushing is a surefire way to miss things that will eventually cause problems. I am often called in to fix a patio that was built on an insufficient base that, while great at first, has become a wobbly mess with failing edges. Ideally, the client wants to fix just a little section, which I totally understand. The problem is that a good fix is hard to do by simply pulling up a few bricks or pavers and resetting. We usually have to remove and reset a large portion or even remove the whole thing so we can build the proper base first. And that is where the hard work lies.

Some common planting mistakes are selecting the biggest plants at the garden center to get that instant finished look or buying too many plants and planting them too close together or too close to the house. This fast work of buying what is pretty to your eye in the moment or what seems to fill the space on planting day doesn't mean it is the correct long-term choice.

It takes time to build things well. It takes patience to nurture plants into their full expression. The best projects are those that have the appropriate amount of time and money allocated to them, so that each step unfolds as a thoughtful process.

BREAK YOUR PROJECT INTO SUBPROJECTS TO MAP WORKFLOW

Divide your project into smaller subprojects so you can see the development unfold in small manageable sections or parts. Think of it this way: it is ideal to develop, build, and plant what you can see by standing in one place. By that I mean, you don't want to be juggling details about the front yard while you are in the midst of building the back yard. It is distracting to do it this way, and distraction means critical elements may get overlooked. I see this result often with DIY projects. If you are embarking on a project, keep the scope narrow to improve your precision and increase your success. If you are going to hire contractors to do your work, having a keen sense of the segments of your project will help you decipher quotes and gauge progress, especially when you are developing a master plan for an entire property.

Subprojects are the features and layers of a larger project. For example, if you are renovating your entire backyard, which includes building a patio, a planted privacy screen, several ornamental gardens, and a lawn and irrigation system, then you can consider each of these to be the parts or subprojects of the larger backyard renovation project.

Then take one big subproject element like the patio and break it into segments of construction. When building a patio, your overall construction segments would go like this:

1. Excavate the land for the base.

2. Install aggregate stone to create the compacted base.

3. Install the sand or stone dust setting bed and then the paver or stone selection.

4. Apply the edge and joint finishes.

To make sense of this, create your workflow to align with the construction segments and to do that, look at each segment individually. You might look at the first construction segment and start asking questions.

- What's involved in excavation?

- Will I need an excavator?

- How will I get one here, and who will operate it?

- What do we do with all the soil that comes out of the excavation?

- Can we use it, or do we need to truck it out?

Approach each subproject in the same manner.

Next, note which phase of each project is contingent on the completion of the phase before it. If the sprinkler system isn't finished because you ran into buried boulders while laying the pipes in the backyard, then the team that is coming to lay the sod on top of those pipes need to be rescheduled. But to keep the project going, you will shift resources to remove the boulders and place them strategically into the planted privacy screen to serve as a quick redesign to solve a problem and take advantage of this newfound element. The point is to plan really well to make it easier to handle the inevitable hiccups. It does take extra work up front, but you will save time and money in the end. An added bonus is taking advantage of design tweaks that can improve the overall outcome. It has taken me many years to become proficient in thinking through all the potential construction scenarios and even with more than thirty years of experience under my belt, I still work a project down to the very last detail so that every moving part is clearly mapped and I can quickly adapt if something changes. This takes time; there are no shortcuts.

Finally, be sure to allocate additional time and budget for any potential hiccups that might lead to changes in your workflow. I should say, changes that *will* affect your workflow. It amazes me how many changes occur as a project is being built. Changes are common to avoid an unforeseen problem, like shifting weather such as a storm or heatwave, or discovering unwanted debris buried in the ground. You might make changes to take advantage of a newly recognized opportunity, like deciding that you want a shed now instead of later. It was on your WANTS list and you thought you would be willing to wait, but now that you see the work happening you say to yourself or to your landscape professional, "Hey, I think I want to get my shed now. Can we do that?" To make sure that you can do what is needed, build contingency time into your estimated time budget. That's maybe 20 percent above the estimated time it would take if everything went exactly according to plan.

IDENTIFY THE HARD-TO-REACH SECTION

Select the farthest and most difficult section to reach in the landscape to work on first. In other words, go to that corner of the property that you can reach only by running over the other sections of the landscape. This may be the area of least interest to you, but it should still be the first area you tackle. If you wait until later when more interesting areas are complete, you will have an access problem. Reaching this difficult spot will require running over something you just built, which is no fun and it is not cheap.

For example, one of my clients had installed a pool using a pool-installation company, which was understandably only concerned with the pool itself. After it was fully installed with the pool deck in and the fence up, they called me to see if they could hire my company to landscape the area behind it to improve the view from the house overlooking the pool. They always planned this as phase two of their project. Why? Because to them, the pool was the project! The glaring problem to me was an utter surprise to them. I had no physical way to reach that area with the machinery we needed to do the work they desired. We could cut down mature trees and remove a few sections of fence and drive over the new concrete pool deck to reach the back, but all I could think was, *I don't want this job!* And I didn't take it.

Starting with the section of your project that is hardest to reach is not only a great tip for DIY, but also, if you are partnering with professionals for your project. Remember, the pool company is only thinking "pool." They aren't thinking of the whole landscape. You must, must, must dive into the discussion of what comes first in your project development if you want to avoid these kinds of disappointments. This upfront planning is a win/win for both the landowner and their professional partners. It allows setting a clear vision while also inviting the evolution of the dream as time unfolds each segment of the project!

CREATE YOUR SCHEDULE

Now that you know where you are starting on your landscape project, the timeline for that first subproject, how much it will cost, your workflow, and who is doing what, your next step is to start the scheduling process. Six main elements, all of which take time and space, need to be taken into consideration when scheduling projects of any size:

1. **Purchasing**. Locate all your materials, select the right materials amidst all the options, and then purchase

them. Allow for the time it will take including when you will need these items. For example, maybe the pavers you want may not be available until you are six weeks into the job, so you'll need to plan for that.

2. **Mobilization.** Allow time to gather all your tools and equipment and to make sure you have the fuel you need for that equipment. There may be travel time to and from a project area to consider.

3. **Project staging**. Clear an area to put all the purchased items until you are ready to use them. This includes pallets of pavers, lumber for decks, cubic yards of gravel and compost, and equipment. This area is where you will "park or put" all your tools and where you will stage the waste and debris pile. Take time to pre-plan for that space use. Or maybe you don't have an area large enough to hold compost and pavers, so you have to plan to have the compost delivered after your patio is set. As you acquire materials, plan for accessibility to the products you need first so you can get to what you need, when you need it.

4. **Production.** Calculate the actual building. This part is the one most everyone is familiar with and thinks about when scheduling whereas the other five elements usually get short shrift. When scheduling production, think about these factors:

   · **Demolition.** What might need to be removed before you begin your project, such as an old concrete patio that needs to be jackhammered?

   · **Foundations.** What in your plan needs a base, footing, or foundation belowground?

- **Installation**. What are the best practices in the industry to guide you in your installation?

- **Finishes**. What work is left to do when the bulk of the installation work is complete? What resources do you need on-hand as soon as you complete the installation?

5. **Project Clean-up**. This is one of the most important parts of the job. At my company, out of respect for the client and our craft, daily clean-up time is woven into every single job. We never leave a job site a mess. You always want to maintain a neat worksite. A neat worksite is a safe and efficient worksite.

6. **Demobilization**. Build in time to follow best demobilization practices. Every day, put everything away clean, sharp, and oiled for the next work day. Recycle as much of the waste as you can whether it is paper, plastic, metal, and so on. Allow time to stockpile extra materials neatly or be sure to remove them from the site so you don't end up with a junkyard.

For activities 3–6, I want to mention land protection as an underlying directive. You have seen constructions sites and can probably conjure up the look of them: stuff everywhere, trucks and equipment parked all over the land, every inch covered with the elements and debris of construction. That does significant damage to the soil in the form of compaction. When planning each of these activities, set your intention to do the least amount of harm you can to the delicate soil strata beneath the surface. This will pay you back in the end by ensuring that your land rebounds well from all this activity.

Each one of these elements of the project takes time to plan and complete, so you need to schedule every step. Keep in mind that time has a monetary equivalent that includes the cost of your time or your landscape professional's time. By pre-mapping the unfolding of the project on a calendar you can develop a reasonable and realistic estimate of how long this endeavor will take from start to finish. Remember to add a fudge factor of about five to ten percent for weather and product delays. If you are partnering with multiple contractors, remember to factor in a time cushion for their own delays too. I have learned from experience and from some hard knocks that it matters who has control of this schedule and project flow. A danger to watch out for is dividing things up so much between contractors that there is no longer a lead project manager. Whether it is you or a contractor of your choice, it is a good idea to charge someone with the schedule and project control. This central command will keep you sane and your project on target for completion close to your agreed-upon deadline.

CREATE A PROJECT FLOWCHART

Make a flowchart that starts at that farthest, most difficult section of work and list the second, third, fourth, and so on sections until you have the whole project mapped on a timeline. A simple, inexpensive paper calendar works great for this. I buy those big 18- x 24-inch ones from an office store for a few bucks. Then, using colored pens and sticky notes, I build my project timeline in a visual way. Those small sticky notes let me move things around until I get it right. This timeline will give you a clear visual for how your project will unfold. I think this part is kind of fun. Understanding this before you begin will give you a real leg up on steps 4 and 5, which take some effort and thought to develop.

Calculate the Financial Investment Needed

Before you start your project, it is always a good idea to understand the financial investment. To understand the financial investment, the design process must be finished. That doesn't mean you can't tweak later; you just need a solid scope of work to price out.

If you identify with the Actor avatar, then calculating your project before you start building is absolutely necessary for your peace of mind and success. If you are the Audience avatar, the contractor will handle all of the calculations for you and manage all necessary subcontractor cost for you, and together you will, of course, discuss budget. You may not need this section beyond a peek into how the numbers are developed. If you are a Director avatar, you will need to be clear about what you are doing yourself versus managing. If you are managing several subcontractors (acting like the project general contractor) then you have several contracts to review and understand. I will put out a small cautionary note here: while you might want to calculate costs for a project on your own as a control tool—for example going to the supply store and pricing out the square footage of pavers you are going to need for your patio—I advise against spending too much time on it. There is no way for you to accurately estimate the tradesperson's costs to build a project—beyond those paver units—so it could take you off course. Again, budget must be discussed, but as a landscape designer/contractor, I would run from a client who handed me a spreadsheet and told me what the job should cost. However, being familiar with what is involved in the scope of the project and the overall estimate is really smart, so we'll review that here.

To calculate costs, you need to break the project into its smallest parts to estimate quantities in units. You want to know:

- How many hours will each step of the project take?

- How many "parts" are necessary? That is, you will need to create a list of materials, the units needed, and the price per unit.

Think of this process like making chocolate chip cookies. You determine the quantity of ingredients you will need such as flour, eggs, butter, sugar, vanilla, baking powder, chocolate chips, and maybe nuts. Make a list. Price it. Then, determine the time it will take to get your project done following steps 1 to 6. This approach to piecemeal estimating is by far the best way to get to a real price.

As you break down your project, think about the following categories:

- **Plants**. Determine what you are putting where, make a list, and then price each and every item.

- **Materials**. Create a list of what items you will need, how many you need, and attach a cost to each item.

- **Equipment**. Create a list of the equipment you will need, the time you will need to pick it up, fuel for the equipment, and possible repairs.

- **Contractors**. Meet with your contractors, discuss your project, and collect estimates. This also means hiring the right help to assist with assessing the site, project planning or designing, or doing the entire job.

- **Transportation**. Calculate the cost of pick-up and delivery for all materials.

- **Support items**. Research and obtain necessary permits.

You might not be able to fill in all these categories up front. For example, you will need to determine who is going to help you build your project and get quotes from them before you can figure in the total cost of labor. The point is that you or a contractor will need to calculate each of these items for a total project estimate to be complete.

I would like to stress that you should always feel safe having transparent conversations with your contractors, especially about the project investment, project flow, and payment schedule. Landscape development is much more than gardening, and it can be a big financial leap. Sometimes you have to live with contractors on your property for a long stretch of time. I've met too many homeowners with horror stories of how they felt afraid to approach their contractors with questions or concerns. Please don't accept this for yourself. Find people you like and feel confident being honest with. I call it the "warm fuzzy" feeling. You want to select someone talented and capable for sure, but liking them, even enjoying having them around, is a good thing to look for. Funny as it may seem, I've also coached landscape contractors who have shared horror stories of working for clients who freak them out at every turn. Uh-uh, no good. I tell them not to accept that working environment. Run! Contractors and homeowners should fundamentally get along and have a mutual respect for one another. This ensures a far better outcome.

There's a saying that rings in my head from my childhood. My mother taught me that "Good accounts make good friends." After so many self-employed years, I can say with full certainty, she was right!

Ballpark Estimates

Before you begin your project, you want to gain some insight into how to measure for a ballpark investment. For instance, is your project a $2,000 project or a $20,000 project? A $50,000 project or a $250,000? Getting clear about your ballpark is a great place to start assessing your investment.

A dependable method to get to a ballpark investment level for a residential master plan is to take the current market value of your house and property and multiply by 30 percent. This number will generally cover a functional landscape with many of the standard elements we think of in a home landscape such as a lawn, gardens and trees, maybe a patio and a walk, necessary grading, drainage and a watering system, and screening for privacy.

Worked into actual numbers, we can estimate that:

- Owners of a $300,000 home could spend $90,000

- Owners of a $500,000 home could spend as much as $150,000 for a complete landscape

- Owners of a $1 million home could easily spend $300,000 for their landscape

These numbers may seem either high or low to you, but they are "in the ballpark." And remember, I am not talking about simply adding a garden. I am referring to integrated landscape construction. These numbers don't make a distinction about what you will be building, but rather suggest this investment level is both reasonable and probable given the home you own and the value placed on functional outdoor living in our present culture. Additionally, we aren't talking postage stamp-sized lots or umpteen-acre sites either. This is a reasonable ballpark for properties of roughly one-half to one acre. When considering these numbers, it is important to note that a functional outdoor living space adds value to your property so if the project is done well there will be a return on this investment when you sell your home. You could spend 20 percent or 40 percent and get closer to your comfort level and cover all your personal needs, wants, and wishes, while addressing the property constraints and necessities. Plus, there are many variables that will affect this ballpark estimate:

- What elements and features do you want in your landscape?

- What hurdles and challenges do your site conditions pose for your project goals?

- What part of the country do you live in and how are expensive materials and services in your region?

Many professionals are a little nervous about the term "ballparking," because once money enters the conversation, things invariably get sticky. For example, let's say that during a discussion about my company building a patio for you, I tell you that a patio of the size you are considering could cost between $15,000 to $20,000. What number do you think you or most people will focus on? Yup, the lower one. And that number sticks like glue. But here is the thing, ballpark estimates are extremely rough guesses of your potential investment. They are just to give you a frame of reference. What you want from a professional is to understand the range you are in. There is a big difference between a $20,000 project and a $50,000 project, and it would be nice to know that in advance.

It is important to understand that you use the ballpark estimate to get an idea of your potential costs so you can determine how to proceed with your project. If you find that the landscape investment of 30 percent of the value of your home works for you, and you have only about half of that to invest, then you will most likely be phasing in your project, tackling one part at a time. And that is totally okay. That is a viable and reasonable approach. The trick is to be honest with what you have to invest in time and money and then craft your project to be well suited to those resources.

Estimating Myths

There are a couple of myths about how to estimate a project. The first is "materials times three." The second is the "square foot" method. Both of these approaches make assumptions about the simplicity of installation and tend to miss the subtle nuances and not-so-subtle hurdles that each unique project may present. And to be sure, every project has some unique elements that will drive costs beyond these two estimating methods.

I am not saying you should never use these methods to determine your project investment. But you should take the outcomes with a grain of salt and understand there may be flaws in the estimate because of missing critical build components. Let's untangle those myths.

Materials Times Three

This industry trick works for small or singular elements, but starts to unravel when applied to larger, more complex projects. Let's look at this method when applied to installing a tree. You multiply the retail cost of a tree by three to get close to the installed price, which will include the necessary planting materials such as loam, compost, and fertilizer. This method works well if transport, access, and installation are all straightforward. But if issues arise with any of those three parts, your real number will quickly surpass this estimate.

For example, if you have to pay someone to transport that tree for you rather than picking it up yourself, that will cost more. If you don't have direct access to the location, like on a hill in your backyard, that will be harder to access than if you were planting it in the front. When you go to plant the tree and you dig a hole and find nice soil, you are golden. But if you hit compaction, rocks, and sand, a job you thought might take two hours could now take four.

Additionally, this method doesn't translate to all projects. When you try to apply this method to a patio and calculate the cost of the paver units or natural stone times three, the estimate is way off and far less than what it would actually cost. All the other pieces such as the standard transport and delivery, access and staging, site preparation, installation, and disposal far exceed the remaining two-thirds cost the equation allows. Add any hurdles or hiccups in this process and the variance between the sum of the tripling method and the actual cost can be quite wide.

Square Foot Method

This industry trick can work when the site conditions are textbook how-to, easy and predictable, and the unit of cost per square foot takes into account *all* the variables of a standard project. Do not take the cost of the paving material only and multiply by three because it just doesn't work!

To calculate the cost of your patio project, take the cost of a finished patio with all materials, all labor and various other costs and divide the total by the number of square feet of the finished project. Here are a few breakdowns:

- One 500-square-foot patio using natural stone with a finished cost of $35,000 translates to a cost of $70 per square foot.

- One 500-square-foot patio using a concrete paver with a finished cost of $25,000 translates into $50 per square foot.

The average cost between these two patios is $60 per square foot, which may be a reasonable benchmark for pricing a patio assuming the site conditions and designs are similar to the example patio.

The hiccup is that every site is different. Some have a stable mix of sandy/rocky soil that will be well suited as a firm patio base, requiring only light excavation and base preparation. Another site may have many feet of loam with a high amount of organic matter, which requires a far deeper excavation and base preparation to get a base stable enough to withstand temperature fluctuations. When sites are nice and flat with great access and stable subsoil, that patio may be under the $60 per square foot price. While sites with a substantial access issue and grade challenge, in combination with deep loamy soil, may be well over the $60 per square foot price.

Keep in mind that estimating a project takes a good deal of attention and practice. Rushing is not advised. Just like rushing the build process can produce poor results in the final product, rushing the number crunching can be a road to surprise costs. These costs can blindside and disappoint you with what is commonly referred to as "budget creep." The exercise of breaking a project into its parts will help you quantify each element and feature so that you can make sense of that final number.

***

This exercise of determining your project development plan, mapping out all of the players and parts, scheduling the timeline, and outlining the investment will give you a sense of clarity when you need it the most. Confidence is king when it is supported by solid planning. You are ready to build! But hold a moment. As your project gets ready to come to life, it would be wise to take a little time to think about how to care for what you create, so keep reading. All aspects of the landscape need care including the masonry, woodwork, metalwork, concrete, asphalt, and lighting. But no aspect requires care as much as the plants. This is an important topic to learn before you start your project. Part IV is devoted to the stewardship of the horticultural elements of your Life-Scape.

 TODAY'S TASKS

1. Decide who's building this project. Will it be you or will there be partners and who are they?

2. Schedule the duration of the project. Do you have time to do the whole thing, or will time constraints mean that bringing help is a good idea?

3. Outline the investment for this project. Are you

confident in that number? Will you build all at once or in phases?

4. Identify the contingency plan for weather delays or other unforeseen conditions.

PART IV

STEWARDSHIP

You are an integral part of not only the birth of your landscape, but also of rearing it to a vibrant maturity. Your partnership with your landscape is a protective, nurturing, "forever" relationship that will evolve with time. In Part IV, I will discuss the actions and behaviors you need to adopt to care for your landscape during its three critical phases of becoming a permanent and long-lasting element of your property. Acclimation, establishment, and stewardship. In these final chapters, you will find tips on what to look for, what to anticipate, and where to turn for help.

8

INITIAL SURVIVAL

"It helps us to focus on the ecosystem as an integrated functioning unit, and it deemphasizes the conservation of a single species. Surely this more comprehensive approach is the way to go."

—Douglas W. Tallamy, *Bringing Nature Home*

You are done. The last blade of grass is in place. Now what? You are going to focus on your plants and their initial survival. Here is the super cool news: plants will grow whether you nurture them or not. They want to grow. They don't *try*, they just *do*. And, if they become totally stressed-out, they may fail to thrive or even die. Assuming you keep their stress at bay, your plants will live. Plants simply strive to live. They don't get depressed or moody about life. They are wonderfully simple in that regard. The trick is not just helping them live but setting up an environment within which they will thrive—lush and green, flowering profusely and beautifully, and withstanding the ebbs and flows of Mother Nature's mood swings.

Your nurturing and care will be the difference between a plant living versus thriving. To ensure this flourishing state, you want to front-load your efforts into the two to three years of its initial survival. Plants cared for in this way during this initial survival period will tend to have a strong constitution and resilience over time. During the stewardship phase that follows the initial survival phase, you will have to do less and less to ensure they live, to the point where you need do *very little, if anything* to ensure life.

The initial survival period consists of two phases:

- **Acclimation (duration: 12–18 months).** Your plants are recovering from the shock of being "uprooted" from one home and moved to another. The plants are just trying to stay alive. Some plants can look rough in this stage. Your job is patience and unwavering care. Don't give up on them.

- **Establishment (duration: 12–18 months).** In this phase a plant community has made it through the acclimation phase. It is no longer in shock. The plants are "getting along." They are showing signs of recovery and healthy growth. Their growth is still slow, meaning it isn't up to the pace of fully established plants.

The phases of the initial survival period may be easier to remember using this old gardener's adage:

- First year, they sleep (acclimation)

- Second year, they creep (moving from acclimation to establishment)

- Third year, they leap (establishment complete)

By the time the first two stages are complete, your plants are fully at *home*. It is all about growing and reproducing. Their number one goal is owning as much real estate as possible and making lotsa babies.

Acclimation

When you go anywhere new, you have to acclimate to your surroundings. If the change is temporary, maybe a vacation where you are entering a paradise of sun and warm breezes, acclimation is most likely pretty easy, especially if getting to your destination was relatively painless, and when you arrived you had the resources you needed at your fingertips, such as nearby restaurants and sunscreen close at hand. You can pretty much just lie back and sink into a temporary change meant for nothing other than rest and relaxation. In this case, you will make a fairly smooth transition over a short period of time. If your trip got off to a rough start with plane delays, car trouble, and missed connections, acclimation might be a little tougher. Still, if your destination environment is soothing, your trip will be relatively carefree after your rocky start. You will recover quickly.

If it is a bigger change of environment, like moving to a new city or starting a new job, acclimation is a little harder. You have to figure out dozens of details to find comfort. In addition to adapting to a new environment where every task involves a learning curve, there may be unforeseen factors which increase the odds of a less-than-smooth transition. What if your new job is not what you expected in the beginning, with lots of office drama, or your office isn't ready, so you have a temporary desk in a hallway? What if your furniture and clothing boxes arrive two weeks late, leaving you in an apartment with no furniture, none of your favorite clothes, no kitchen equipment, and sleeping on the floor? The list could go on. All these upsets make acclimation harder because stress increases with each unsettling incident.

These types of scenarios are far from life threatening; they are simply discomforts of the mind and setting. You have food and water. You have contact with loved ones. You are safe.

Okay, let's move back to your plants. I understand humans are different and more complex than plants, but stress is stress, and it is well documented that whether you are a human being or plant, stress can be a deterrent to well-being. When stress is repeated, elevated, and stems from a threat to or lack of resources central to basic survival needs, it can be a killer.

When plants are moved, they are literally uprooted from their homes and placed in a foreign environment. Whether they have been dug up for the move or have been sitting in a nursery waiting to be moved, they are in a transitional state of waiting. Once moved, they experience three stressful events:

1. Being physically removed from the place they know as home. This means that they have had a violent destruction of biomass because their roots have been cut off. Container growing has reduced this stress but not eliminated it.

2. Being transported in a vehicle. Keep in mind that plants are not biologically equipped to travel. There's a lot of jostling around, tying up, covering and cramming together to get a plant from point A to point B. This amounts to physical handling that isn't "normal" to a plant.

3. Being placed in a new foreign environment that is completely alien to their experience thus far in their

lives. Even when you attempt to match conditions, it is still new and different to each individual plant.

It is important to understand how stressful these three events can be for a plant. This awareness will equip you to make sound decisions about how to make each event as stress-free as possible, beginning with doing everything you can to avoid and reduce the severity of shock to the plant.

AVOIDING AND REDUCING SHOCK

From the moment you plant the plant until the moment it is not endangered anymore in the first 30–90 days, your plants are recovering from a very high-stress situation, much like a state of shock for a human. You will be doing triage. Your job is to baby those plants, and to watch, watch, watch. I don't mean you have to puddle them with water every five seconds. What I do mean is that you must be in communication with the plant, your contractor, or your designer, or all three. You can triage by making sure that everything you do both before and during the installation of the plant is correlated to the lowest possible stress and the lowest possible shock.

- **Proper timing.** Not all times of the year are appropriate for all activities. Planting is particularly sensitive to the time of year. Be clear on what you want to accomplish, and whether the weather is right for your activity. For example:

    · Do not divide and transplant plants in the summer— it is usually much too hot.

    · Avoid planting at all in the highest heat.

- Don't plant in high mud times of the year.

- **Proper plant, proper place.** Choose the right plants for your location so that they can easily "feel" the fit and start the healing process quickly. I've listed a few key points here, but this is a broader topic that you will want to investigate further, including specifics of your region and the plants you are considering.

  - *Choose native plants when possible.* They will still be stressed by the move, but to a lesser degree because they are already related to the ecosystem you are working within. They are more adaptable to the fluctuations in the weather and insect communities, making their acclimation and establishment periods shorter. However, treat them with kid gloves at first because they can suffer stress just as any other plant can. One of the biggest mistakes I see is a wanton neglect of new native plants caused by a misconception about their immediate strength and resilience. There is a misguided idea that since a native plant selection is technically from your ecosystem, they somehow don't need any care from you. This is not true because as I mentioned, stress is stress. The babying is still needed; it's just for a shorter duration.

  - *Place plants with the end in mind.* Plants grow, it's that simple. Do your research to know how big and how fast plants grow. A common question I get from clients is, "How big will it get?" My answer is almost always, "Too big!" especially when we are discussing foundation plantings. While knowing the ultimate size and pace of growth is useful, it is equally useful to understand the effectiveness and relative difficulty or ease of pruning the plant. Remember, this is a managed landscape. It isn't a natural occurrence in nature. You are blending nature with your whim and design and asking, "How long can I make this fit and still have vibrant plants in a healthy ecosystem?"

· *Plant good companions.* Design is certainly about combining form, texture, and color to create a pleasing aesthetic, but when you are working with plants there is something more. There can be a symbiosis among plants. A simple Internet search will generate long lists for edible plant companions such as vegetables, herbs, fruits, grains or even ornamental plant companions in the Rosaceae family coupled with alliums, plants in the Ericaceae family, coupled with ferns. The list goes on. Ken Druse wrote a whole book about it called *Natural Companions: The Garden Lover's Guide to Plant Combinations.*

· **Pair plants and the elements.** When making decisions about what plants to install, consider exposure to sun and wind; soil types such as sand, silt, or clay, and level of organic matter present; and water needs such as dry to low water, moderate water, to wet conditions. You may combine plants that love boggy soils in a wet area of your landscape. Or combine plants that are wonderful bedfellows in sandy, hot locations. Sometimes you can even support pollination by choosing plants that will support insect development through the seasons.

Think of the butterfly life cycle: the caterpillars need host plants for habitat and leaves as a food source, while the adults need nectar plants.

- **Proper planting.** Take care in how you plant. Do not stuff plants into the ground. How would you like to be rough-handedly squished into a new environment with no support network? Yeah, not so much. Don't do that to your plants. Take the time to prepare the planting area to receive the new plants. That can mean soil testing, amending, digging nice wide holes, clearing out weeds and invading roots, and so on. Select healthy, robust plants from the start from reputable growers and resellers who actually care about plants.

  - Putting a dollar plant in a nickel hole is the worst thing you can do. Your plant will fail to thrive. Especially if that planting practice is followed with neglect.

  - You *can*, however, take a nickel plant and plant it with great love and care in a dollar hole, nurture that plant to a higher state of health, and get a win.

- **Best practices.** Best practices are plant-specific. You can find plant-specific information by searching the Internet. Many botanical gardens and plant associations have produced useful planting information that is free. Each state has a land grant university that will also have actionable information for you. Just type in "land grant universities <your state>" or "best practices <name of plant>." Often you will find that very good plant nurseries will also produce high-level plant care information.

- **Proper transport.** Plants must be protected when you transport them from the nursery to their planting site. Cover them, tie them carefully, and pack them neatly. Plants are stationary lifeforms so travel is novel to them. Be gentle and kind. That means no trees hanging out of trunks or standing up through sunroofs. Yes, I've seen both! You don't even want plants stacked in the back of a pickup without cover. Think of being on the highway in the back of a pickup with no shirt, no hat, no sunglasses, no coat, going 55 miles an hour. Now picture that for a 25-minute ride in the direct, hot sun. How's your skin feeling?

    - Sustained 55-mile-an-hour wind is an intense weather pattern that most plants cannot survive, not even when they are planted.

    - Plants don't even like 30-mile-an-hour winds. Think of it like swaddling a baby. Ideally, when transporting, cover them with a cloth or burlap plant tarp, which you can purchase at a good nursery or online through nursery trade suppliers. Plastic doesn't allow for airflow that the plants need to breathe. And plastic increases heat, which can also be damaging.

- Good sources—use reputable nurseries and growers. You can buy at big-box stores but beware and inspect everything. Your best bet is to purchase on the specific store's delivery days, which are the days new stock comes to the store. You have the best chance of plant material being in its very best condition.

- The bottom line is, paying more for plants is often directly correlated to the growing practices and care given to the plants as they await sale.

- A specialty vendor is geared toward producing and tending the highest quality plants. The extra money is worth it when the source is reputable, helpful and engaged in your success.

All these practices help get you started with well-supported plants that "hit the ground running." Your new plants will feel good almost immediately in their new location. They may even feel liberated within days—no more ball and burlap, no more pot- and rootbound feet. They are happy.

TASKS TO TAKE CARE OF DURING ACCLIMATION

Two critical-care tasks need to be front and center for the first twelve to eighteen months of your new plant's life in your landscape: watering and weeding.

Watering

No matter how well you do all the of the preceding, your plants *will* need water. If you have an automated system it can make watering easier, but it can also do great harm. Avoid the "set it and forget it" practice of installing an underground irrigation system, setting it to run, and never checking. As the weather cools down or rains, you might not need to water as much. The opposite is true in a heatwave or drought, when you will need to water more. Also, different areas of your property have unique drainage patterns. Different conditions such as exposure to sun and wind mean you will have wet areas and dry areas. Setting and forgetting an automatic waterer is expensive in two ways: you often use more water than you need, and you often lose plants from over- or underwatering.

Plan to hand-water *and* monitor your system performance every week for the first few months after planting. If you are monitoring weekly and you notice a dry patch by one or more plants, instead of just dialing up your irrigation system as your first fix, think about adjusting the angle of delivery and augmenting your system with hand-watering until you get the irrigation right. Or maybe your dry patch is because of exposure, slope, or competition from tree roots, in which case you can water by hand to help the plants that aren't getting enough water. After that, you can start looking at it monthly. From there, you will monitor seasonally. Eventually, you will need to monitor only two to three times a year. For more about watering practices, go to *www.TheGardenContinuum.com* and search *watering* in the Landscape Blog.

Weeding

One thing is a given in any garden: weeds find their way in, always. So just be aware and be ready for action. Regular spot weeding is the best way to avoid infiltration. And before you start, ID your weeds. That is, know what a weed is and is not. To tell the difference, you need to know your plants. And keep in mind that not all new sprouts are weed invaders. Sometimes they are your thriving plant successfully sending off seeds that are germinating because you did such a *good* job picking your plants. At my house, we always find baby Dogwoods and Viburnums. My husband loves to nurture these seedlings; then, when they are big enough, he moves them to a desired location and continues to nurture them. Of course, at some point you have too much of a good thing, and these little seedlings need to be removed to keep your landscape in order.

An important note of caution: inspect plants at the nursery for weeds in a ball-and-burlap (for trees and shrubs) and in pots. High-end nurseries have rigorous plant monitoring policies that ensure a low weed presence in the plants they sell. It is impossible to be 100 percent weed-free without lots of chemicals, so your first job is to weed the plants as you are installing them. Pull weeds out of rootballs and out of plant pots before you plant them. For more about weeding practices, return to my website and search *weeding* in the Landscape Blog.

Keeping a close watch on watering and weeding during the acclimation phase sets up your plants to move successfully into the establishment phase.

A Word about Weeds

I am sure you have heard the definition of "weed," which is "anything you don't want in your garden," but that is not entirely accurate. Often, we pay good money to add plants to our garden that get called weeds, so I've broken down what constitutes a weed into categories.

Annuals. This type of weed goes through its full lifecycle in one year and produces hundreds of thousands of seeds that will germinate readily in the landscape. Crabgrass is one that we love to hate.

Perennials. These weeds live many years, have one seed cycle a year, and germinate readily. They also return yearly because they develop a root mass if they're not removed.

Turf grasses, vetches, and many ornamental perennials and herbaceous plants fall into this category. Dandelion is one that is hated openly by the conventional turf industry.

Volunteers. This is a general term used to identify ornamentals or plants in the surrounding environment that have seeded in the landscape. Seedlings from maple trees and many other trees and shrubs fall into this category. There is less hate here, but certainly lots of misunderstanding. Take rose of Sharon, for example; it self-seeds like there's no tomorrow!

Invasive Species. This is a distinct designation for plants that have been deemed dangerous to a specific environment. They can create an allelopathic environment, which means they create chemical and biological changes in the soil that will kill other plants. Garlic Mustard in the Northeast is an example. Or they are space invaders in that they will literally outcompete other plants for resources. Norway maple and Japanese knotweed are two examples that have been targeted with increasing levels of vilification.

Establishment

To move from acclimation to establishment, you need to monitor and lower one element from the equation: stress. As long as excessive and repeated stress is part of the equation, your plants cannot establish themselves. Let's say in the first year you baby your plants. You give them the best care. Then the next summer, you neglect them. Maybe you have a heatwave or drought, and because you are not watering them enough, their stress level increases. As with humans, after a while that stress wears them down and makes them weak, thereby making them less resilient over time.

The goal is to get the plant out of stress from transplanting, environmental pressure, or competition and then keep it out of stress as it establishes. In the acclimation phase, the plant is just trying to stay alive. It isn't sure about this new place. In the establishment phase the plants says, "Hmm, this place is pretty cool. Think I'll throw down some roots." In this process of setting feeder and stabilization roots the plant is actually setting itself up to grow and really live in this place. Keep in mind that there are normal stresses in life for humans as well as plants. The trick is to build tolerance and resilience through supporting the development of health and vigor so that moderate and intermittent stress can be managed with low to no input from you in the future.

The establishment phase takes place between twelve to eighteen months. The plant needs to live through a full growing season after acclimation in order make it through establishment, and then on to stewardship.

TASKS TO TAKE CARE OF DURING ESTABLISHMENT

You are still going to be watering and weeding, but it feels less "desperate." The plants have some staying power, and they are filling in and starting to keep weeds down a little. Now, in addition to watering and weeding, you will add pruning to your list of tasks.

Watering

After acclimation, your plants will have more roots. This

means they will have the ability to take up and store more water. Additionally, if you are mulching properly, and caring for the soil correctly, you will have an active soil-life community that is also assisting in stabilizing water in the system.

With all that, if a drought is predicted you can offset that by making sure to manage proper hydration. Simply put, you want to avoid having stressed plants going into a drought; they won't handle it well. Strong plants can take a dry spell and come out of it without much loss or damage.

The point with water is to achieve balance. Finding that balance takes visiting your landscape often enough with a critical eye toward hydration and tweaking when necessary. If this isn't your thing, make sure you partner with a landscape care provider that can manage this for you. It sounds complicated, but it is not. The critical action here is monitoring.

The whole world of water is changing. We are more aware of its value and scarcity as our cities and towns grow in population. Water bans, once a rare occurrence in the summers of my early gardening years, are a commonplace restriction in my area during the spring straight through the summer season. Irrigation systems, once reserved for the wealthiest homes, are now found in the most modest of neighborhoods. We are overusing water in the landscape to offset damaging construction and poor horticultural practices. To compound this truth, our overwatering is also damaging our water systems, including our aquifers and waterways. By employing best practices around soil management, plant selection, and ecosystem development, we will be able to use less water and keep that water clean.

Weeding

After acclimation, your plants will start to grow, especially the herbaceous ones. Ideally, you have a heavily planted system, which is the best way to squeeze out invading weeds. At this stage of your landscape development, your goal is to make sure that weeds don't invade any plants. It is easy to see weeds that pop up in the spaces between plants and to pull them out. However, often the weeds that pose the biggest problems are the ones that take up residence close to, under, and in the desired plants. You must check *in* the plants, *under* the plants, and *around* their bases to make sure there aren't weeds hiding and taking up residence. If you don't check on your plants, you will miss these weeds at first, and in time, they will develop a root system entangled with the desired plant making extraction difficult—and sometimes impossible.

Vigilance is your friend! Once you learn to spot one of these sneaky invaders it will be like magic—all of a sudden, you will see them everywhere and be able to extract them.

Pruning

Pruning usually starts during year two. Let me be clear. By pruning, I mean cutting the plant in a way that is appropriate to its growth habit using hand-pruning tools, not hedge shears or electric or gas-powered tools. The exception might be when you are shearing a formal hedge, but even then, I am suspect of the use of these tools because they tear through plant tissue in an uncontrolled fashion that causes unnecessary damage. The plant will have to work hard to recover.

The goal of pruning in these early stages is to manage the uneven or gangly nature of plant growth when the plant is just starting to grow. Through pruning you can correct uneven growth spurts, remove crossed or twisted growth, damaged growth, or spent flower stems.

You are not managing size yet. You are just guiding growth by managing initial form and shape. Nothing more. It shouldn't take much time at all to prune in the establishment stage of growth.

As you move into the stewardship phase, beyond the third year, you will notice that the plants begin to thrive and grow at a much faster pace. This is when you'll begin to manage for size as well as shape. If you started this work early in year two, then the following years will be easy as you guide the shape of your plants while they grow.

Practices to Avoid in All Phases

During all phases whether you do the gardening yourself, hire out specific jobs, or have a team of professionals take care of everything, you want to be aware of, and avoid, these pitfalls:

- **Overwatering.** The characteristics of overwatering or underwatering are the same: your plant looks droopy and yellow. To determine whether your watering practice is in need of tweaking, check the soil to see if it is too wet or dry. Let me be clear, by "check the soil," I mean you have to actually touch it with your bare hands, maybe even dig into it beyond the top few inches so you can get a good read. Look for wet areas that are gluey, sticky, muddy, or smelly. Dry conditions might have a moist top layer with soil below that is sandy, caked, hard, and stiff. If you are overwatering, let the soil around the plant start to dry out, and then adjust the amount of water you give that plant in the future. While overwatering or underwatering a few times won't kill a plant once it is established, unchecked, it will kill a plant during the acclimation and establishment phases.

- **Letting plants dry out.** Again, you want to test the soil by physically touching it. If the soil is dry and hardened, the water might be running off rather than being absorbed into the soil. In this case, you might dig a moat around the root ball to capture the water and let it sink in. Or install a soaker hose to allow a slow seepage of water into the lower sections of the soil. Remember, if the top of the soil feels damp that does not mean the soil below that where the roots are living is hydrated enough, especially if it's a new plant. Take the time to gently dig in a few inches to see if you are getting proper infiltration to the depths needed to properly hydrate your plants.

- **Letting weeds go to seed.** Clearly, if you let weeds go to seed, those seeds will spread all over your yard. A single dandelion can produce 15,000 seeds per year! But those seeds don't go away in one season. Every time you deposit seeds in Mother Nature's seed bank, she pays you interest. Big time. How can she be so generous? She hangs on to your money and invests it. She won't give out more seeds than can germinate. Everything else, she holds onto for up to seven years. There's a farmers' adage: one-year of seeds, seven years of weeds. If you let your weeds go to seed one year, you can be guaranteed that the plant will provide seven years of weed seed.

- **Adding too much mulch.** Avoid piling too much mulch

over the soil or mulching too close to the root collar, which is the area between where a plant's main stem or trunk turns into roots. A good rule of thumb is to spread mulch about two to three inches deep and keep it about two to three inches away from the collar. This is where the micronutrients are super-active, the water is super-active, and the oxygen exchange is super-active. If you mulch too deeply, you are suffocating the oxygen exchange and limiting the ability of water to get to the soil microbes and the plant roots. This suffocation can give rise to a whole host of other biological and predatory problems.

- **Letting lawn invade beds.** The overall composition of your landscape is defined by the edges between one thing and another. If you let your edges get blurry, your landscape gets fuzzy, making it less compelling. To keep the landscape "managed," you want to keep your turf grass out of your beds and definitely out of your plants. Maintaining strong edges is a very good practice to keep your landscape looking maintained and functioning well. It isn't an effort to be overly formal. It's an effort to support clarity between the growing environments while reducing your work and your potential losses.

Staying on top of your plant care and making sure you follow best practices will help you avoid costly mistakes and will help your plants and your landscape composition thrive.

***

As you move beyond establishment beyond the third year,

your plants will begin to grow at a much faster pace. This is when you manage for size as well as shape. If you started this work early in year two, then the next years will be easy to guide the shape of your plants as they grow.

 TODAY'S TASKS

1. Determine your water source and research the costs of added consumption, whether that is a direct cost (dollars for water) or the added draw on your well's capacity.

2. Research your town's/city's water-use rules. Does your municipality enact annual water bans? If so, what is your work-around solution?

3. Consider the care requirements for new plantings through the acclimation and establishment phases. Have a discussion with your contractor or suppliers about product guarantees and any restrictions or limitations on those guarantees.

4. Research local gardener support. Who are the available partners that could help you with horticultural support?

9

FOREVER TWEAKING

"Life holds more meaning when the past ties in to the present. When this happens, one gains assurance that the present will also tie in to the future."

—Robb Sagendorph (1900-1970), 11th Editor, The Old Farmer's Almanac

Congratulations! You did it. Your plants are established and thriving. All your features are built. You love being in your yard. Chris and I spent so many years working on our landscape that the sense of accomplishment was a transient emotion. We would finish one area and feel great about it, only to shift our focus to the next phase of work. Then one day, there wasn't a next phase! I remember it perfectly. We finished the patio that had been three years in the making and bought comfy furniture for it. Then we installed some low-voltage lighting. Those first few months with the landscape finished were surreal. I would come home and walk the landscape, taking stock of all the inviting elements in our yard. It was so pretty and so cozy, just like that initial dream I had about what it could be like.

This feeling is the goal; this is what you are aiming for, a feeling of accomplishment and of pride in what you have created. And while the intense focus of acclimating and establishing your plants is behind you, your landscape still needs your involvement. It is not done. There is no such thing as "doneness" in a landscape or with any life form. Are you done?

With all of the elements of our vision in place, we keep making tweaks and adjustments as things mature and change. That's because our vision evolves as our life does. To this day, Chris and I continue to work in our landscape as a part of our commitment to this super cool environment that is our Life-Scape.

This final stage of your landscape stewardship is an enduring process. It is a lifetime commitment. As steward, you have the obligation to manage, nurture, and guide. This stage is all about the long-term care you will provide your landscape in the form of correcting failures, managing water and soil, caring for plants, monitoring insects and disease, and following a succession plan as the landscape matures and changes over time. This may be something as simple as pruning and as involved as removing a tree that has simply started to decline with age. You may do the work yourself, or hire landscape professionals to do it for you, but you need to be aware of what this stage entails to ensure enduring success.

The way to do that is to develop a relationship with the natural systems that are our landscapes, so that you become keenly aware of how they are faring over time. The simplest way to do this is to regularly walk through your landscape. I know, sounds too simple to be useful, but I promise this action is powerful in two significant ways:

- If you walk your landscape as little as once a week,

you will notice changes from week to week. Many of them will be fun to watch, some may give you pause or concern, like, "Hmmm, what's going on here?"

- If you walk more often, three times a week to even daily, you will not only become intimate with the complex development and evolution of your landscape, you will also be doing a great service to yourself, to your energy, your stress level, and your immune system. A ten-minute walk in nature has great power to calm your nervous system and give your busy mind a rest. Bump that up to twenty or thirty minutes from time to time and the health benefits, such as lowered heart rate, deeper breathing, and a general sense of well-being in the moment, will increase. And you will be "seeing" your landscape. Noticing it in different times of day, season, and year. The combination of your communing with nature and your awareness about your very own landscape is what truly turns your landscape into a Life-Scape.

As you cultivate this walking awareness, you increase your understanding that everything is systems-oriented. Everything is connected. By building this type of relationship with your land and landscape, you can better withstand the constant pummeling of the next fad, the next trend, and latest application for a greener lawn, or the latest product to kill bugs that may actually be necessary to your ecosystem. Then if you have issues with the caterpillars snacking on your maples, or a bit of anthracnose showing up on your Dogwoods in springtime, or the emergence of a little red thread in your lawn, rather than reaching for the next product to apply, you will assess the issues with systems in mind. You will be motivated to ask good questions. Is that plant in the right place? Did that plant suffer from drought stress last year putting it into a weakened condition over the winter, making it susceptible to that insect or disease in the spring? Shift to the assessment of issues, problems, and opportunities within your landscape. See it through the lens of how it is connected to the bigger picture of its environmental experience both past and present. You will come up with better answers and solutions for both the present and future.

As for opportunities to build or add to your landscape, perhaps you are thinking about a gazebo because gazebos are everywhere on digital idea sites and every garden store you walk into. Before you build the structure, assess the function, the placement and the reality of your lifestyle before jumping in. It is better to realize you will never use it than to build it and think, "Oh, look at the interesting folly that I am never going to sit in" every time you look out the window. Or it would be a lot better to realize you will use it a lot and bump up your investment to the next size to gain the full effect of the structure, rather than be bummed in the first week after you install it because it is a bit too small. This is a common disappointment when cost is the only decision driver.

You can see that systems thinking is not only critical to the health of your ecosystem, it guards against wasting money or knee-jerking into projects or actions that aren't going to serve you, your landscape, or the environment at the highest level. The truth of landscape development for most of us is that we purchased a "used" landscape. There is usually a house already there, with many years of life in the landscape behind it. A select few of us are able to start fresh on a raw piece of land where we can dictate every structure, location of trees, blade of grass and flower petal, but that isn't the norm.

What we have is an inherited ecosystem that we need to respect before we dive into altering it. While we may be able to alter it somewhat, there may be some flaws inherent in the land we purchase. Flaw may be the wrong word; it may be perfect for nature, but out of alignment with our vision. Being able to identify these flaws and make immediate or later decisions about them is part of stewardship.

When Chris and I bought our home, the previous owners had planted several blue spruces along the driveway we called the runway. We wanted to move the trees as a part of moving the driveway. The previous owners also planted native dogwoods (*Cornus florida*) in the full sun, which is not the preferred location for this species, so we moved those too. These tasks were easy to do upfront with a machine while the plants were still young. Our woods, however, were a different story. We knew they were likely too close to the house, but we didn't have our vision clear enough in those early years to make a real decision about what to do one way or the other. Then about fifteen years in, we noticed some intense ant activity at the base of several pines and oaks that were close to the house, and we made the decision to cull about thirteen very large trees from our property. We were extremely hesitant to take so many trees out early on, but once we did the work, we were thrilled with the new light and the positive growth we saw in just a few years in the younger woodland trees. And we had tons of oak firewood for our wood stove!

Another aspect of the stewardship phase is identifying failures such as plants that previous owners planted in the wrong place or need to be removed for safety. In new landscape developments, failures will generally show up in the first three to five years. These failures might be plants that have been planted too deep, plants that become overwhelmed by insects, or plants that do so well that they start to crowd out their neighbors. But some failures often don't show until the plants are years into maturity and are more expensive to correct. For instance, trees with poor branching that weren't pruned early on and then break in a storm, or a tree planted too close to the driveway that starts to block cars or lift the paved surfaces.

If you follow what I have laid out for you in this book, I hope that any failures you have are small ones that may be induced by an environmental fluke. And that would be great. Or maybe you got this book late in the game and already have some problems to address. For you, now is the time to identify them and correct them, because the longer it takes you to notice or address a problem in your landscape, the more costly it will be to correct.

Retain Vibrancy: Why Hydration and Nutrition Matter

The easiest way to think about health in the landscape is to correlate it to human health. Everyone knows someone who is vibrantly healthy. They may have a super healthy diet and a committed exercise routine. And you know, when you are eating well, drinking the proper amount of water, and exercising regularly, you feel better. I know I do. It is not subtle either. When I have a period of time when I drink more coffee than water, I feel less energized, caffeine aside!

As with all biological life, health comes from that life form having the optimal conditions available on demand. That would be nice, but we also know it isn't always possible. With our own bodies, sometimes we have to make do with less, so when we have access to more water, for example, it is a good idea to take in some extra hydration to catch up. I am not saying that more is better. I am suggesting that when a state of lack can be followed by a little extra TLC, biology is wired to rebound into health, provided disease hasn't set in.

WATER MANAGEMENT

This is no longer a task that needs your attention in the ways you gave it in the early years of your landscape. Basically, the biggest plants will need the least water support over the long term. Native plants will generally be the strongest and the most resilient in managing drought and temperature swings in all these categories. Here are a few tips:

- **Large trees.** Both evergreen and deciduous large trees will become self-sufficient provided they were planted properly and in the right place.

- **Understory trees.** Both evergreen and deciduous understory trees will also become quite self-sufficient in time, but they may need attention in times of extreme drought.

- **Small woody plants.** Evergreen, broadleaf evergreen, and deciduous small woody plants may need moderate assistance, depending on the type and age of the plant. The larger and more native the plant, the less attention it will need. Exotic, marginal plants living on the edges of the woods and the field with exposed or dwarfed selections may need more watering in the long term, especially during droughts. Proximity to large and understory trees will also create deficiencies in water access due to neighboring root competition that may need to be addressed.

- **Herbaceous plants.** There are so many types of herbaceous flora available, it is impossible to determine their long-term water needs. Choosing the right plant for the right place is the single most important decision you can make when putting in herbaceous plants. They are smaller and have fewer resources available to them over the long term than their woody brothers and sisters. Hybrid selections and exotics can have questionable survivability and a little more variability in water needs.

Water is limited because it is a finite resource. It is neither created nor destroyed but it is moved around and limited within systems. When more people drink from a closed system it will deplete. If you take 10 people trying to drink from the water resource flowing into a 20-unit apartment, and then you increase that number of inhabitants to 100 and then to 1,000 people but the resource doesn't increase, at some point there isn't enough water to drink and recycle back into the system in time for the next person to have a drink of water. Water availability is dependent on a system of recharge and recycling within the system. Time is an integral part of that equation.

We all need to be collectively mindful about how we water our plants. In addition to natural rainfall, you have four water delivery systems to choose from.

- **Hand water.** You grab a hose or watering can and hand water, what I call direct-delivery watering. You are literally taking the water and putting it on a spot and delivering it. This option works well when you have a specific plant that needs added attention. Always watch the water to make sure it is soaking in and not running off.

- **Sprinklers and soakers** (manual and manual with timers). These are manual systems that you hook up the soaker hose or hose to a sprinkler, water for two hours, and turn off the water. With the hose and sprinkler, you may then move the system, and repeat. Or you might attach a hose timer to your faucet to start and stop the watering in one area, before moving your sprinkler to the next. These old-fashioned systems are mindful, affordable, and a good choice for establishing new trees, new lawn areas, new planting beds, or just keeping up an area that has suffered from previous neglect. The idea is that once your plants are established, you won't need this system any longer.

- **Irrigation systems** (automated and underground). An irrigation system makes it easier for you to deliver water, but it can also make it easier for you to waste water. It can also pollute water by picking up nitrogen and phosphorus from lawn fertilizers and depositing the water in storm drains and waterways. It can kill your plants by giving them too much or too little. On the other hand, irrigation systems are getting better and better. The great advance in irrigation is its adoption of the WaterSense program, an Environmental Protection Agency (EPA) water use monitoring system that was developed for plumbing that is now being applied to irrigation. These systems can save an enormous amount of water through low flow water emitters and controllers that allow you to program detailed environmental conditions as well as link to weather stations. These smart controllers are replacing conventional or dumb controllers, which have no connectivity to the condition of your environment. You will also find sprinkler heads that reduce water use, similar to low-flushing toilets. Irrigation technology has grown by leaps and bounds. With that said, if you have an irrigation system that is over ten years old, it will need updating to incorporate these conservation-minded advances. Additionally, no system should be set and then left unchecked. This "set it and forget it" mentality is wasting massive amounts of water around the globe.

- **Rainwater recovery** (rain barrels and underground tanks). Rainwater recovery is super important, and there are oodles of methods for rainwater collection. Many cities also have methods for collecting grey water, the relatively clean waste water from baths, sinks, washing machines, and other appliances. There are regulations in many areas about how you are allowed to do this, so be sure to check with your local water department to get guidelines on these tools.

SOIL MANAGEMENT

The health of the soil is vital to the health of the ecosystem. There is no escaping the reality that if you have unhealthy soil, the entire system will be weak. Compacted soil as the result of unchecked construction practices is a good example of unhealthy soils devoid of functional life. Managing the soil food web is a surefire way to keep health in the soil, which will then support the plants. For your plants to thrive, you want to continue to test your soil every three to five years and record your findings. That way you will have a record of the chemical profile and be able to supplement your soil if needed.

There is no need for regular or regimented feeding of old landscapes if the soil is managed properly. *Teaming with Microbes: A Gardener's Guide to the Soil Food Web*, by Jeff Lowenfels and Wayne Lewis, is an excellent resource for building and keeping your soil healthy. Lowenfels also has a book called *Teaming with Nutrients* if you want to dig even deeper into this topic.

Controls—Insect, Weed, and Disease Monitoring

Managing the state of health for any living organism, such as your pets, means you feed them well, give them water, provide good shelter, and love, and expect they will fare very well. Since you know all biological life can get sick or be challenged by a parasite, you are vigilant in noticing signs of sickness. You want to be vigilant about your plants as well. Holes in leaves, defoliation, discoloration of leaves, holes in bark and trunks, ooze from bark, and pretty much anything that seems off is worth investigating. Integrated pest management (IPM) is an ecosystems-based practice for monitoring and testing for insects and disease in a landscape to apply targeted controls only when needed. To learn more about IPM in your area, consult a land grant university as well as plant associations that service your state.

As mentioned, the specific sciences of insects and disease are huge fields of study and not my area of expertise. As a designer, contractor, and steward of the landscape, I first strive to balance the system through right design and plant selection, conscientious construction, and careful stewardship. When I struggle with problems beyond my ability to effect change, I partner with specialized professionals. If it finally comes to considering some controls, partnering is critical. If you want to find your best partners, you can:

1. Go to a reputable garden center where you can consult with landscape professionals.

2. Check with an organic, ecological, or gardening association, like the Organic Landscape Association, the Ecological Landscape Alliance, or the Master Gardeners Association.

3. Consult your local land grant university.

I highly recommend that you focus your research on organic health practices and controls over fast synthetic applications of products. It is my belief that these quick and dirty applications cause more weakness and rob the system of resilience over time.

INSECTS

There are always new bugs to worry about, but if we are working within the ecosystem then there are often good bugs that will manage the "bad" bugs, so the system is balanced. Bugs aren't inherently bad. There is, however, a co-evolution that happened between insects and plants so when you have a really good vegetative balance, there is generally enough food to ensure that no bug ever ends up being bad enough for you to go after with the big guns. Of course, this doesn't include invading and introduced species with no co-evolutionary history with your local flora.

Many bugs will chew your plant leaves, because your plants' leaves are their food. Of course, if the insects get out of control, you may have to step in. You don't want to put up with total defoliation that threatens plants because we also have a duty in the managed landscape to help plants survive. But a few lacy leaves are not a threat; we can live with them. Look at caterpillars. Most of them turn into a moth or butterfly, and the only way they can make the transformation is to eat leaves when they are young. If you want to protect Monarch butterflies, but you also want to do away with all insects that eat leaves, you are going to be stuck. In the book *Bringing Nature Home: How You Can Sustain Wildlife with Native Plants*, Douglas Tallamy does an amazing job explaining how bugs are integral to our ecosystem, and how we are dependent on them for our survival. There is no way I can begin to summarize all the points in his book, so I recommend you add it to your reading list.

Now, this is not to say that things will never get out of balance. Balance isn't a finite destination; it is an ongoing process. The trick is to manage any imbalances in eco-conscious ways. That is why selecting native plants, considering soil health, and applying integrated pest management are super important. That way, we make sure we are not going on random killing sprees that endanger all those really fun moths, butterflies, and caterpillars that don't do bad things.

WEEDS

As with insects and target treatments, it's constructive to have the same mindset with weeds and avoid spraying toxic weed killers everywhere if possible. This is why integrated weed management (IWM) is so important. Integrated weed management is a long-term approach to controlling weeds using several techniques. It involves the physical techniques of mulching, hand removing, and cutting; the chemical technique of rotating herbicides; the biological technique of introducing a weed's natural enemies; and the cultural technique of selecting hardy, vigorous plants, such as natives.

Combining techniques helps reduce the chance of a weed building a resistance to one technique, as it might with continued use of an herbicide. Again, your local land grant university or organic land care association can help you determine the methods best for your area. Over time, IWM should reduce the weeds themselves and the seed stock in the soil without harming the ecosystem.

It has taken years, but I've finally established my company practice to fully exclude the application of any weed-killing products. It is a mindset, and it takes vigilance and attention. Planting and mulching are central to my company's success and hand weeding will always be a service we provide to our clients.

DISEASE

Getting sick is part of the life cycle for all living organisms. Just like we know that eating sugar all day long will likely make us sick and weak, the same is true for plants. If we feed them synthetic water-soluble fertilizers all the time, they become weak and possibly succumb to disease. The best defense is to make sure your plants are healthy and strong through proper hydration, nourishment, and management.

To help your plants stay healthy, avoid these practices that weaken your plants and soil and can give rise to disease:

- **Improper planting** — either too deep or too shallow, leaving burlap wrap and cages on plants, or planting in the wrong place altogether

- **Improper watering** — either too much or too little, planting in a location that is too wet or too dry for the plant's preference

- **Improper soil management** — compaction, overfertilization, over-control of insects and weeds with chemicals

- **Improper exposure** — too sunny, too shady, too windy, too cold, too hot, stagnant airflow

The Maturation Process—Keeping the Design Intent Over the Long Haul

In chapter 6, I discussed the four stages of the landscape lifecycle: new, managed, mature, and aged. The direction of your stewardship care will differ based on where in this lifecycle your landscape falls, so you want to keep track and provide the necessary care accordingly. Succession planning, garden edits, and plant choices are critical to maintaining your original design intent throughout the lifecycle of your landscape.

SUCCESSION PLANNING

Without any environmental disturbance such as fire, flood, or earthquakes, plants will keep succeeding from one type to the next, each succession eventually killing off the layer before it. This is the way of nature. For more on how you can work with natural succession, I invite you to go to *www.TheGardenContinuum.com* and search the word *succession* in the Landscape Blog.

When Mother Nature intervenes by shaking up, burning, or drenching the planet, she knocks succession down toward the early stages of life, ensuring that our planet isn't completely covered in forest. On the same note, without these events or human intervention, your landscape will naturally become forested land. When there is no disturbance, succession in the landscape follows a simple trajectory from herbaceous, high-bacterial environment to a woody, high-fungal environment. But we do intervene, so we create the disturbance over and over again.

Every time we mow our lawn, we disturb the grass plants. We are knocking succession back down the ladder by saying to our grass, "Do not grow tall. Do not make seeds. Stay exactly as you are." Mowing our lawn is a managed disturbance, which is much different from a natural disturbance, such as when a fire blazes over a field of grasses.

The difference is this: the natural intervention is infrequent and often bold, covering huge tracts of land unlike human intervention (unless you are talking about clear cutting forests...and that is another discussion all together!). Now, I don't want you feeling like mowing your lawn makes you a bad steward of your landscape; it doesn't. Regular lawn cutting to a desired height for ease of use is simply a design choice. When you understand that this recurring action taxes the turf grasses' resources, you will (hopefully) have more patience with the care the lawn needs to stay vibrant and lush.

Here is another way you might intervene in succession in your yard. You have an old row of sugar maples that line one side of your driveway that are starting to die because of age. You really love sugar maples in that location so you may look for a safe and appropriate location to plant a few new sugar maples while the old ones are still there. That way, you could start replacing those older trees as they die off, a few at a time. The young ones will grow in a protected location until they go through establishment, then you can cut down the big ones and let the new ones take over the post.

I hope you can now see how important your intervention in succession is to maintaining your design intent and keeping your yard vibrant and healthy.

LANDSCAPE EDITS

Land isn't a static entity. It moves with the seasons, expanding and contracting with the ebb and flow of heat and moisture in the atmosphere and in the ground. These movements shift the setting of all hardscape features. In New England, this is highly evident by the cracking of concrete and mortar over time. It is inevitable.

As your yard matures, caring for your plants will become less about whether they live or not, and more about how big you allow them to get. You may not want them to get so big that they undermine the original design intent. Your goal is to ensure that you preserve that intent over time, allowing it to evolve but not fail. Making changes or edits to the garden is what ensures that a gardener's life is *never* boring. When I talk about garden edits, I am referring to the process of assessing your gardens, your overall landscape, and your hardscape elements every year. You want to be clear about what needs attention, and then make changes, updates, or repairs to maintain your design intent and keep your plants vibrant and healthy.

Once your plants are established, you will bump up against opportunities to make changes, tweaks, fixes, or additions that will make the landscape even better than before. For example, you create a beautiful entry to your property. You started with a mailbox and a lamp post next to your driveway, and that was it. Then you decide to make a huge bed around them, and you plant a weeping cherry, some roses, and daylilies. The first year you spent most of your time weeding and watering. As time went on, you weeded less, and then later, you watered less. Time goes by, and the cherry tree has grown and hangs so low it covers all your roses. You want the canopy, so you prune a lot off to keep the tree where it is while pruning those branches up to let light into the roses. Then, lo and behold, one summer your roses don't do very well. It is hot, so you figure the heat is getting to them, and you begin watering again. Now you realize that these roses have to be watered *every day* because they are always wilting or turning brown. Maintaining roses in conjunction with the root system and natural branching pattern of your maturing cherry tree is monopolizing your time.

Now you have an opportunity to edit. Maybe you create a new bed on the other side of the driveway, move your roses, and add a few perennials. After a while, your daylilies are looking pretty raggedy, so you dig them up, divide them, replant some under the tree on the very edge of the canopy and move the others to another bed. By making these two edits, you are maintaining the intention of your design and you still have a beautiful centerpiece calling out to the world, "Here's a beautiful home. Come drive by my cherry tree up the drive to my house, because everything in my home is beautiful and inviting, just like this."

By editing, you are maintaining your intent of a beautiful entry. Holding fast to the original plan could mean losing your intent. Your entry is no longer inviting when people drive by and all they see is a broken-down cherry tree with its branches dragging on the ground and dead, decrepit roses, and nasty, wilting daylilies. You have to go through the editing process to make sure you keep the vibrancy while the planting composition is succeeding. You edit as your garden matures after five to seven years, and again at eight to ten years. This is the process of the garden edit.

What Type of Edits Will You Make in Your Mature Landscape?

- Dividing herbaceous plants
- Replacing plants
- Moving plants
- Removing plants
- Adding plants
- Expanding bed lines to accommodate your plants as they grow
- Shrinking bed lines to reduce workload or create more room for lawn or recreation areas
- Retrofitting watering and lighting systems as watering needs may change as your yard matures, and lighting may need to be adjusted as your plants grow
- Restoring hardscapes

PLANT CHOICES

Landscapes will often mature to sizes much larger than we desire. Unless you live on a palatial estate with gobs of room for plants to grow to full maturity, pruning will be a constant in your life. The truth is that none of our plants really fit in the residential scale. They are not designed to grow no taller than a first-floor window, stay within the confines of a three-foot bed, or to not shade out the understory plants. Generally speaking, your plants are all going to eventually be too big if left untouched, so this is how we end up needing to develop high-level pruning skills. Planning for growth when you first design your landscape is critical. Choosing dwarf or compact plants, creating larger than needed beds in the beginning of the project, and positioning plants with growth in mind will reduce the need for aggressive pruning in the future.

Know your plants and always opt for pruning when plants are young to guide their mature shapes. That way, when you prune a mature plant, it will be more surface and less structural. Not all plants need the same kind of pruning, nor do they all respond to pruning the same. Pruning is a true art form that is informed by plant morphology and growth rates. To become proficient, you must learn your plants and practice with patience and humility. That means *no hedge shears!* This isn't a how-to on pruning so instead I offer you this pruning summary to help guide your actions.

- **Growth rate.** There's a real difference between a plant that is growing one foot a year and one that is growing one inch a year, so pruning is very different. If you take two inches off a privet hedge, which can grow a foot to a foot-and-a-half every year, you are not doing much. Whereas with an Alberta Spruce, which only grows an inch a year, you may not want to prune at all. So, growth rate matters!

- **Bloom times.** You want to be very mindful of when the plant sets its buds. For instance, if you prune a rhododendron in the fall, you are cutting off all of its spring blooms, so it is much better to prune in the spring after the flower die. Other plants, such as spirea, sets buds on new spring growth, so you can prune it early in the spring (or in late winter). Bloom time is key.

- **Best pruning times.** The rule of thumb is right after a plant flowers. You can search the Internet to find the bloom times and the appropriate times to prune each of your plants. This is where botanical gardens, plant and gardening societies, and land grant universities can offer great training information.

- **Best pruning methods.** The plant's growth habit is the first indicator used to guide you to the best pruning method. For instance, forsythia and rhododendron have very different growth habits and thereby very different pruning requirements. Also, it is necessary to understand nuances within plant types. For example, just knowing it is a hydrangea isn't enough; you have to know the *kind* of hydrangea. Knowing this helps you to differentiate between whether it is an old-wood-blooming hydrangea or a new-wood-blooming hydrangea. Start by knowing the genus and species; you must go beyond common names in this stage of your learning. Then find out whether the plant blooms on old wood or new wood.

- **Best pruning tools.** Here's the bottom line: if you paid $15 at the local hardware store, it is probably not a great tool. It may last for that season but if you are really investing in gardening, then look at what the pros are using. Have you ever used a really good knife in a kitchen? Ah, heaven. Then you pick up a junky knife and try to cut a tomato. Yuck! It is not rocket science. Good tools make a world of difference in your experience and outcome. You also want to learn how to care for your tools. Cleaning, for example, is imperative. Would you want your doctor to use an instrument on you that had just been used on another patient without sterilizing it? That is gross! You have to clean your tools from time to time. You don't have to clean them between use on every plant, but if you have a sick plant, you must clean your tool before you go on to a neighboring plant or you run the risk of spreading that pathogen.

***

In these final two chapters, we have covered a great deal of juicy information about nurturing your plants throughout the three phases of your landscape lifecycle. The key point of this chapter is that by developing a relationship with our landscapes, by developing a forever partnership with these natural systems, we become keenly aware of how they are faring over time, and by doing so, help ensure enduring success.

TODAY'S TASKS

1. Check your irrigation system's age and function. Consider hiring an irrigation company that offers Irrigation System Audits to come assess your system.

2. Check your landscape for rainwater runoff. Consider installing a rain barrel or two to collect excess water. Research the functionality of a simple water chamber to put rain water back into the ground. A good resource is NDS Stormwater Management Solutions.

3. Do a property walk and list out the mature elements that you'd like to keep that may need some professional support. Ask yourself what could use some moderate edits to amp up performance.

4. Download my free eBook to get more fine gardening tips. Visit www.TheGardenContinuum.com and click on Services and select Fine Gardening for access to the eBook.

CONCLUSION

THE GARDEN IS AWAKENING

After reading this book, I hope you made two major shifts. First, you moved away from a linear mindset where solutions are based upon products and moved toward an experiential mindset where solutions are based in non-linear systems thinking, which is a process. Second, I hope you gained an awareness of the intricacy of our environment and how to work within it. I am not saying you need to immerse yourself in all the science involved. I am saying it is really important to be aware of the complexity of this system we are working in and approach the system with humility and at a slower pace than the commercial industry has trained us to do. When we approach the landscape in a systems-thinking way, we inevitably create a partnership with that system, one that begins to feel easy and natural.

Chances are you will make some mistakes. I've killed stuff, sometimes by accident and sometimes on purpose. All professionals, really all people who grow plants, kill some. I planted roses when I was an apprentice only to see them fully plowed under and crushed in their first winter. Then there was the Asiatic lily garden that became ravaged by red lily leaf beetles, so rather than poison and kill them, I ripped them all out. I've also chosen plants poorly, like planting a river birch on the corner of a porch about twenty-five years ago that "ate" the porch and had to be taken down after just ten years. It is okay, but I won't make that mistake again!

I'd love for you to walk away from this book embracing the idea that gardening requires resiliency, and that you want to be really smart about what is okay to experiment on in your landscape, and what you need to get right the first time. It is one thing to say, "Gee, I wanted to try a trout lily in this filtered sun under my birch tree because all indications were that it would work really well here. But I am noticing that it is getting long and leggy and floppy, and I hate it here, so I am digging it up because I can see the birch roots are choking it out." But it is not smart to apply the same experiential philosophy to your patio. There is an exact method to building a patio, and it isn't buying pavers and sticking them in the dirt. That is destruction, not creation. Rectifying a poorly laid patio isn't nearly as easy or inexpensive as transplanting a trout lily.

Throughout this book, I discussed the organization and management necessary in a Life-Scape to create and maintain plant health and the integrity of your design intent. I also discussed the third element of a Life-Scape, the *wow* factor, what resonates with and pops for you. Remember, a Life-Scape is personal. It is about you, your family, your life, and the current stage of your life. They are transformational. You will make changes in your landscape to reflect the way your life evolves.

It is my hope you will understand that investing your time, your energy, and your money in the development of the land that surrounds your house is an invaluable investment in how you live. It is an investment in your health and your well-being, as well as the health and well-being of your family, your pets, and your environment. Ideally, this book will also give you the information and tools you need to develop partnerships with expert service providers and resources. There is no way to know all you need to know to reach perfection. Collaboration and partnership between homeowner, contractor, gardener, academic, and trade resources along with embracing the reality of time and evolution as one of your partners will be the real key to making your own Life-Scape a reality.

For me, the partnerships I have made and nurtured with clients, fellow contractors, vendors, and educational associations have kept me going all of these years. So many of the people I have met through my career have become respected friends. I can honestly say that I love my work today as much as I did 15 years ago and plan to 15 years from now. I am encouraged by nature and inspired by the cutting-edge advances that my industry makes each year. It is my sincere hope that my love and respect for this work came through these pages and inspired you to take charge of your project with humility and confidence. I wish you the best success. Garden on!

APPENDIX

Frederick Law Olmsted - Arnold Arboretum https://www.arboretum.harvard.edu/library/archive-collection/historical-biographies/frederick-law-olmsted/ - pgs 48-50

Richard Louv - *The Last Child in the Woods* - Chapter 1 - pg 26

Daniel Pink - A Whole New Mind - Chapter 1 - pg 32

UMass Extension

https://ag.umass.edu/resources/home-lawn-garden - pgs 34, 116

New England Wildflower Society's GoBotany https://gobotany.nativeplanttrust.org/ - pg 34

Missouri Botanical Garden. http://www.missouribotanicalgarden.org/plantfinder/plantfindersearch.aspx. - pg 34

Rachel Carson - Silent Spring (1962) - pg 50

Ernst Haeckel, a German philosopher and professor (2/16/1834 – 8/9/1919) - The History of Creation - pg 61

Howard Odum, an American Ecologist (9/1/1924 – 9/11/02) - Environment, Power, and Society - pg 62

Ludwig von Bertalanffy (9/19/1901 – 6/12/1972) - General Systems Theory - pg 62

Douglas W. Tallamy and Rick Darke - *The Living Landscape: Designing for Beauty and Biodiversity in the Garden.* - pg 63

International Concrete Paving Institute (ICPI) - pg 83

Accredited Organic Land Care Provider (AOLCP) - pg 83

Department of Environmental Protection - pg 87

Wetland Bylaws - pg 87

Betty Edwards book *Drawing on the Right Side of the Brain* – pg 94

Craig Smallish - Artist - free-association process - pg 95

Ken Druse - *Natural Companions: The Garden Lover's Guide to Plant Combinations* - pg 189

Jeff Lowenfels and Wayne Lewis - *Teaming with Microbes: A Gardener's Guide to the Soil Food Web* - pgs 57, 213

Jeff Lowenfels - *Teaming with Nutrients* - pg 213

Integrated pest management (IPM) - pgs 213-215

OLA - Organic Landscape Association - https://theola.org/ - pg 214

ELA - Ecological Landscape Alliance https://www.ecolandscaping.org/ - pg 214

Missouri Botanical Garden's Plant Finder - pg 34

MGA - Master Gardeners Association https://www.ahsgardening.org/gardening-resources/master-gardeners - pg 214

Douglas Tallamy - *Bringing Nature Home: How You Can Sustain Wildlife with Native Plants* - pgs 183, 215

Integrated Weed Management (IWM) - http://integratedweedmanagement.org/index.php/iwm-toolbox/what-is-integrated-weed-management/ - pg 216

NDS – NDS Stormwater Management and Drainage Solutions – www.ndspro.com – pg 225

UMASS Home-Lawn-Garden https://ag.umass.edu/resources/home-lawn-garden - pg 125

ACKNOWLEDGEMENTS

I've been writing for decades in short form—printed newsletters and then a blog, and then two blogs—but I had no idea of the work needed to write a whole book. I've taken many classes on how to write to learn the mechanics of it and yet book writing still felt super hard.

The project took five times longer than expected with more edits and revisions than I could have imagined. It was an eye-opening and sometimes mind-bending experience that I simply couldn't do in one shot or alone. And while I had no grand vision of sitting down and hammering out a book in one fell swoop, I certainly didn't realize how much help and support I'd need. And boy did I need it—writing help, moral support, and loving encouragement to keep going when I just didn't want to anymore.

I had an a-ha moment when a writing teacher asked me a pivotal question. "What's more important, that you write this book, or that the information get out there in the world?" Lisa Tener, my book writing coach, knew that I was stuck on this idea that if I didn't write the book 100 percent by myself, it wouldn't be legit. I was trying to perfect my writing and my understanding of how to write a book to the point where I could do it alone. She shared the reality of solitary book writing not really being a "thing." I will forever be grateful to Lisa because without her wise question, I'd still be brooding over the idea of writing this . . . when I was ready to do it by myself.

Kelly Malone, WordsUp, was my first working partner. With a background in technical writing, she helped get my ideas, experiences, and stories in order. Before working with her, I just had notebooks full of ideas and short essays with no organization. She could see the order in the chaos of my words like I can see order in the chaos of plants. Her mind brilliantly pulled all the pieces of what I had to offer and put them into a structure that made sense and had flow. Together we spent hours talking through each section, recording our conversations and going back and forth about what should come first or last, what should be expanded or dropped. It was magical and took years!

So, all done right? Ha-ha, not so fast. I needed readers! The fear of having my work read was surprisingly crippling. It took me months to work up the courage to ask people to read the manuscript. Finally, I sent out six copies to be read by family, friends, clients, and business partners. Three key readers, Laurie Warren, Rick Fritz, and Maranda Allen, lovingly offered their time to print and read my manuscript from front to back while marking it all up with comments and questions. They told me when I was being too abrupt and bossy, pointed out where I used confusing industry jargon, and cheered me on when I wrote something they felt was brilliant. I will forever be grateful for that amount of time they offered to this work.

Laurie was a constant for me on this journey. She acted as accountability partner, cheerleader and rudder throughout the rest of the writing of this book. Writing her own book at the same time, *Wild World, Joyful Heart*, published in October of 2019, she co-navigated my often-scary journey of putting ideas and beliefs on paper for all to see. We egged one another on, read excerpts, weighed in on ideas, and just kept the fires of creativity going when what we really wanted to do was get a bucket of water and end it already! Thank you, my sweet Beacon Buddy!

I must give a shout out to Dave Orecchio of Bristol Strategy. For the past 4 years he's been diligently working with me and The Garden Continuum to bring industry content to readers of my blogs and eBooks. I am so grateful for his dedication and focused guidance in helping me to develop and deliver on a succinct content strategy so my readers are best served. He's been a major player in keeping my eye on the ball with the development and marketing of this book project.

Finally, my team of super hero editors. Susan Baracco, The Story Architect for Women, was a blessing to align with for developmental editing. She was the one who finally got me to understand how important my voice, but more precisely my tone, was to refine in order to truly reach my reader in the spirit that she'd learned was at the core of my intention for writing this book. She was kind and firm in her comments, a combination I love and can always work with. She was instrumental in empowering me to keep going.

Katie Elzer-Peters, A Garden of Words, is a landscape industry writing, editing, and book packaging pro. She knows both the industry of publishing as well as gardening. Her confident, no-nonsense approach to the process along with her team of editing and creative publishing pros expedited the process of moving from finished manuscript to publishable book with amazing efficiency. Every time I got nervous, she patiently re-explained what was next and calmed my novice mind into trusting her, the process and the flow.

I'd like to thank my silent cheerleaders! My three kids, JoAnna, Maranda, and Bennett for always believing in me and putting up with my scattered parenting when buried in working on this book. And my parents who are both gone now, but offered unshakable belief and loving encouragement in my pursuits.

Last, and most importantly, I want to thank my husband, Chris, for being my life partner and closest friend in all things landscape and family. He probably doesn't understand how critical a role he's played in this process, but without his steadiness, predictability, and unyielding acceptance of who I am and aspire to become, this book may never have happened. His consistent care of our home, landscape, kids, and pets gave me countless opportunities to steal away moments to do the work to make this project a reality.

ABOUT THE AUTHOR

Monique Allen is the founder and creative director of The Garden Continuum, Inc., an award-winning landscape design/build and fine gardening company. Monique hoped this company, founded in 2000, would take all her previous academic training and infield, hands-on experience as a professional gardener, and deliver a new brand of landscape partnership to the public—one that considered the landowner as equally important and pivotal to the success of land development projects, environmental health management, and garden wellbeing.

Monique received her Master Landscape Certificate in landscape design through the Landscape Institute (Boston Architectural College) and rounded out that design training with education in horticulture, botany, and conservation through the Massachusetts Horticultural Society, and the Massachusetts Association of Conservation Commissioners. She sat for nine years on the Franklin Conservation Commission. She's the past president and recipient of the Beacon Award from the Massachusetts Association of Landscape Professionals where she volunteered for two decades to develop and deliver trade education.

She publishes two informational blogs annually—one on landscape designing and gardening topics and the other on operating and developing a landscape business. Her writings have been featured in *American Nurseryman* and her work in *This Old House* magazine. Monique and her company were the lead designers and landscape developers on *Extreme Makeover:*

Home Edition Medfield Project and featured on *The Victory Garden* television show.

Landscapes developed by The Garden Continuum have been awarded for organic landscape development and organic land care. Monique was an instrumental partner in the largest river floodplain restoration along the Charles River in Medfield, Massachusetts, acting as landscape designer, conservation and wetland specialist on the project for the Massachusetts Department of Capital Asset Management and Maintenance.

Presently, Monique continues to run her vibrant landscape practice in Medfield. Each year she teaches a core seminar she developed on Garden Ecology for the Massachusetts Master Gardener Association. She and her team are actively building out the educational arm of her business, called TGC Academy, which is a dynamic landscape and business training platform.

Some of her greatest joys outside of the garden are cooking for and spending time with her family, traveling, reading, studying the practice of yoga, and stand-up paddle boarding.

She lives in Franklin with her family and their menagerie of pets and many, many, *many* plants that live with them on their two-and-a-half acre Life-Scape.

CPSIA information can be obtained
at www.ICGtesting.com
Printed in the USA
FSHW021136280420
69561FS